THE SECRETS OF THE TAROT

ANDREW LAYCOCK

Introduction

It is difficult to put what the tarot means into a simple word or phrase because it means different things to different people. A source of entertainment, a game, a predictor of the future, an omen, a spiritual guide. Which one of these do you think of when you hear the word tarot?

The tarot started as a game, which developed into what we now would recognise as the card game known as bridge. As the world evolved through the middle-ages and into modern times, and people started to question if there was a more profound force guiding us through life, it became a way of helping people tap into their energies to guide them towards their destiny. This spiritual and emotional context became deeper, new decks of cards started to be created with elaborate imagery, heavy with symbolism and meaning. The tarot became a way to predict the future. Psychics, soothsayers and fortune-tellers started to be consulted. Along the way, people began to pass the responsibility for their decisions to other people and the tarot. A whole industry grew up around the tarot, and as it did, people tended to fall into distinct groups of people. Those that believed and those that didn't, those that saw the tarot as a source of harmless fun, those that chose it as a way to live their lives, and those that saw it as unhelpful or evil.

When I tell people that I am a tarot writer, trainer and coach, nine times out of ten, they will react strongly. Depending on their view, I am either someone who has all the answers to their problems, the guy who is going to tell them whether they are going to win the lottery, find a new job, meet the love of their life, or I am a shameless charlatan who preys on people's insecurities and fears. The truth is I am neither. I am just an ordinary guy who has been able to tap into my intuition at a very advanced level, focus my energies on the cards and interpret what they say about a given situation. And anyone, or nearly everyone, can do what I do.

In saying that, people do expect too much from the tarot cards, and it is unfair. Life is what we make it. We cannot and should not place the responsibility for our future on a deck of cards, no matter how much we believe they may hold mystical powers. Whilst it is true that the most common use of the tarot cards at this moment in history is for predictive or fortune-telling purposes, it is unclear how much the accuracy of a tarot reading is down to what the cards say or what we do in response to the reading of the cards. If someone tells us that we are going to find a new job in the next six months, then the chances are we are going to start looking for one. If someone says that we are going to meet the man of our dreams within a year, we start treating the men we meet as potential life partners. I am not knocking fortune tellers or psychics. I know a lot of them and honestly believe that they have a heightened sense of intuition and, in some cases, are able, unlike many of us, to tap into a sixth sense at will. What I am saying is that to expect the cards to tell us what to do or what is going to happen is unfair and doesn't enable us to analyse the decisions that we make.

How I use the tarot, and how I encourage others to use it, is as a source of guidance. An aid to learning more about ourselves or the situation we find ourselves in by looking at the symbolism on the cards. There is so much we don't know about the fields of energy around us, so little of it that we use, that just by tapping into a fraction of it, by focusing on a question we want help with as we shuffle the tarot cards, we can transfer our internal energies on to the cards so that when they are turned upwards, they speak to us. The cards talk to each of us in different ways, and depending on our moods and feelings, we can interpret them differently at certain times in our life. What one person sees another person may not, what we feel one day when we look at a card we may not feel the next. There is no specific meaning set in stone for each card as they are designed to be read in many complex layers and so there is no right or wrong way to read the cards. They are there for us to use as a guide when we feel we need a second opinion on a decision we are going to make, or want to understand how a situation may develop depending on our actions.

Let us take one of the most familiar and instantly recognisable cards in the major arcana, The Lovers. When we look at the card, we see that one of the images is a couple, naked, arms stretched towards each other with an angel hovering above. When one person looks at the card, they may see a couple in love, comfortable in each other's company. Another person may focus on the gulf between them and see that the relationship is just out of reach. Someone else may feel that the dream of being in love is very different from reality. One person may feel nakedness symbolises trust, another naivety, a third passion. Nobody is wrong. What the cards say is correct for each one of us at the time we look at them.

We need to start somewhere, though, when we look at the cards, and in this book, I have given you a broad meaning of each of the cards so that you can start your journey to understanding what the cards mean. However, it is no substitute for handling a deck of cards and studying the pictures yourself. When I am delivering one of my training courses on the tarot, I encourage people to speak out loud when they pick up a card, tell the story that they see, use every tiny detail that is depicted in the card, for everything on the card is there for a reason. My training courses are based on the Rider-Waite deck of cards as this is what I predominantly use unless asked otherwise, but each deck has subtle differences and may emphasise certain details. Broadly speaking, though, the meanings I have given in this book serve as a helpful starting point and provide the general observations of each card.

Most people can learn to read the tarot cards. Contrary to common opinion, they are not the province solely of psychics and fortune-tellers. Reading cards will come more easily for some than for others, depending on how acute and developed our intuition is. The way I learned the tarot, and how I teach it, is by using a stepped approach that encourages people to focus on the mundane aspect of the tarot deck whilst developing their intuition and then moving on to the deeper meanings as they build their intuition. All any one of us needs, to be able to read the cards and use them as a guide in our life, is to combine the intuitive skills we were all born with to the knowledge of the cards we gain to form an educated opinion of what the card tells us. As we develop our skills and knowledge and gain more experience, we can move on from reading one card to reading a combination of cards to provide a detailed reading.

The tarot deck in its complete form comprises 78 cards which are split into the major and minor arcana. The major arcana has 22 cards in it, and these are the cards that have the most powerful meanings and signify long term changes or significant decisions. The remaining 56 cards are the minor arcana, which concentrate on more day-to-day issues. The word arcana means secret, and during the course of this book, we will endeavour to uncover the meanings behind the cards and unlock the door to some of the secrets it contains.

Let us now start our journey through the tarot and see the secrets of life revealed within. There are two ways of doing this. One is to read each section as you look at the card in question. The other is to turn a card over, look at the picture, see how it speaks to you and then consult the book to see how closely your interpretation matches the broad interpretation I have provided. Remember, the cards tell different stories at different times and mean different things to different people. A pack of tarot cards is yours to love, cherish, and respect. They are there to guide you through your life, but they cannot live your life for you, nor should you live your life by them.

The Major Arcana

0 The Fool
1 The Magician
2 The High Priestess
3 The Empress
4 The Emperor
5 The Hierophant
6 The Lovers
7 The Chariot
8 Strength
9 The Hermit
10 The Wheel of Fortune
11 Justice
12 The Hanged Man
13 Death
14 Temperance
15 The Devil
16 The Tower
17 The Star
18 The Moon
19 The Sun
20 Judgement
21 The World

Andrew Laycock

The Fool

The Fool is about to take a step forward into the unknown. He stares at the world around him in happy optimism, unaware that the path he is walking along ends just beyond his feet. His companion on the journey dances at his feet, trying to attract his attention so that he can warn him of the risk ahead, but the Fool continues in blissful ignorance of the danger that he is about to encounter.

Despite the apparent danger that he is in, the Fool is a positive card to draw in a reading. It starts our journey through the tarot and signals new beginnings and opportunities. It does hold a warning, though, that we need to have an idea of where we want to go before we begin any journey. That does not mean we need to be too fixed on one idea that we risk missing any opportunities that life places in our way. We need to be careful that we assess opportunities to identify whether they will help us on our journey or rather distract us from the task at hand. It is very easy to lose sight of our goal, especially if we receive something completely unexpected.

There is a childlike innocence to the Fool, suggesting that when we pull this card, we can be being somewhat too trusting of those around us for our own good. The Fool is lucky to have a faithful companion at his heels to warn him of the dangers of his actions, and this is a timely reminder that we all need someone on whom we can rely. We all know that person, or those friends, who we can trust, and we should never be afraid to ask for advice or support if we feel that we need it. In the same way, if they offer it, we should never dismiss what they say out of hand, even if we do not necessarily want to hear what they say.

The main lesson from the Fool is that we should move forward with optimism and a belief in ourselves that we can achieve whatever we set out to do, but we need to be alert to events that may try and distract us from our goal. We should proceed with what we are about to do but with caution.

The Secrets Of The Tarot

Love

The Fool warns us to be careful and assess whether we have an unrealistic view of what being in love means.

Money

We may feel reckless and want to splurge on something new, but we should be cautious not to waste what we have worked hard to achieve.

Work

This card suggests the start of a new venture or activity, but we should think carefully about whether it is what we truly want.

Andrew Laycock

The Magician

When we meet the Magician, we see that he is holding a staff in his right hand, pointing to the sky, whilst he points down towards the earth with his left hand. On the table in front of him are the tools of his trade, the cup, a pentacle, a wand and a sword. With these at his disposal, he has all that he needs at this time, for he is an achiever who can tap into what he has to get results.

When we draw this card, we are often at a crossroads in our lives and are unsure which way we should turn or where we should go. The Magician is there to remind us that however lost we may feel, we have all the skills and knowledge that we need to be successful. How we use them, though, is up to us.

There are different ways to use the talents that we have each been given in life. We can use them practically and resourcefully, letting each one compliment the other and putting them to good use by making them work together to help us achieve what we want in life. Or we can waste them, by treating each of our skills separately or using one or two to the detriment of others. The Magician is here to remind us that we should be careful not to throw away the skills we have been given but to nurture them, respect them, and utilise them.

We play many roles in life, juggle many balls, have many plates on the table at any one time. The Magician shows us that we can do everything we set out to do, but he carries a warning in common with all cards. If we drop a ball, break a plate, ignore an aspect of our life, then although we may get what we want at this moment in time, we may not, over time, ultimately have what we need.

Love

The Magician reminds us that relationships are complex and that we all have different needs and desires. We should work together with what

The Secrets Of The Tarot

we have to get what we want.

Money

We may need to be creative and look at various solutions to our situation. Money is there, but it will not be handed to us on a plate.

Work

This card signifies that we can achieve everything we set out to do if we use our talents wisely.

Andrew Laycock

The High Priestess

The High Priestess sits on a stone block, the columns beside her representing white and black magic. In her hand, she holds The Torah, and at her feet is the moon. Both contain many secrets and can teach us much. At her back is a tapestry preventing us from seeing what is behind her. The High Priestess must guard the knowledge she holds and only reveal what we need to know.

This card represents wisdom. It reminds us that when we are looking for an answer to a problem, or a solution to a situation we find ourselves in, we should consider what we believe instinctively to be correct and not look too closely for the evidence to back this up. The world holds many mysteries. There is much more that is unknown to us than is known. The High Priestess reminds us that sometimes it is best to trust our instincts and go with what feels right.

When we draw this card, there are forces at work in our life that we know nothing about. The High Priestess often appears at moments of change, when we feel that we are not in control of our life or our destiny. The card tells us not to look too closely for the answer now, for all will be revealed in time when the Universe itself decides that we are ready. The positive aspect of this card is that if we open our minds and hearts, we can meet our full potential. The danger is that if we think too hard and do not allow the Universe to guide us, we risk missing out on all the gifts that we were due to receive.

The lesson from the High Priestess is to trust our instinct and intuition, to believe that even if we don't know why we have come to the answer we have, what feels right can be right.

Love

Our heart holds many secrets, but they will only be unlocked when it is the right time for them to be revealed.

The Secrets Of The Tarot

Money

If we focus too much on money, we risk missing out on the other gifts that the Universe has for us.

Work

Now is not the time to base decisions on logic or a structured approach. Are we doing what we want to be doing, or are we doing what we feel we need to do?

Andrew Laycock

The Empress

I like to think of the Empress as the Earth Mother or Mother Nature, surrounded as she is by all the beauty that the Earth provides, a field filled with crops, a lush green forest and a meandering stream. Although she is in touch with the natural world, her crown of stars reminds us there is a mystical, spiritual side to her. There is more to her than meets the eye.

The Empress represents abundant fertility, creativity, love, affection, harmony, and a mother's nurturing instincts. When we draw this card, it suggests that we are at the start of something new, be it the birth of an idea or a child, a relationship, a new job or any change that we have decided to make. The card serves as a reminder that though we often like to reach our destination as quickly as possible, to be truly happy and fulfilled, we need to care and value what we have at each time of our life. Ideas, changes, new projects, and new relationships need to be nurtured like we would a child through birth, infancy, adolescence, and adulthood. We must not rush headlong through each step but rather take time to enjoy what each stage has to offer.

The Empress is a beautiful card to draw in any reading as she suggests harmony and love in all we are planning to undertake. Still, like every individual we meet on our journey through the major arcana, she has a warning. The Empress tells us that if we do not take the time to enjoy what we have now, we may feel a sense of loss in the future. The present is a gift we should never take for granted nor ignore.

Love

Take the time to value your relationship with your partner, or if you have recently found love enjoy the now and do not try to move it on too quickly. If you are single, the Empress tells us that we must remember to love ourselves before we can truly love another.

The Secrets Of The Tarot

Money

Money is essential in life as it allows us to do what we want and need to do, but money cannot buy happiness. The Empress reminds us to value all that is free in this world.

Work

Success will come through harmonious relationships with co-workers or employees. Whatever we set our mind to will succeed, providing we remember that two heads can be better than one.

Andrew Laycock

The Emperor

In most tarot decks, the Emperor is depicted as an old man, his long white beard suggesting experience and wisdom. He sits with supreme authority on his throne, the ruler of all he surveys, commanding respect and allegiance. His throne is decorated with four rams heads symbolising determination and leadership. The card is the fourth card in the tarot, the number four representing solidity and strong foundations. He holds the Egyptian symbol of life in his right hand, and in his left, he clutches an orb signifying the world over which he rules.

The Emperor is a powerful card to draw. When he appears in a reading, it suggests that we can achieve whatever we set our mind to do through determination, perseverance, and hard work. This does not mean that success will come easy to us, nor that it will necessarily be quick, but if we are steadfast in our commitment to a project, plan or goal, we will achieve what we desire in time. When we get there, our experiences and the knowledge we have gained will ensure our position will be solid and secure.

When we see this card, we should ensure that solid foundations are put in place for a plan or a course of action to succeed, and we should follow the plan methodically and logically. Each step should be carefully thought through and tested, now is not the time for quick decisions based on instinct or intuition. The card warns us that though the road ahead may feel daunting, if we focus on what we want to achieve each day and divide the journey into small, manageable steps, we will achieve more than we ever hoped or thought possible.

The Emperor dominates and brooks no argument but is a kindly and benign ruler, willing to share his knowledge and experience with those he feels worthy. As he provides support to all who ask, we should also look to those in our immediate circle or wider network who may provide us with support and mentoring to guide us on our journey.

The Secrets Of The Tarot

Love

Now is the time to take control. Decisions should be based on a precise analysis of the facts, and we should not let emotions get in the way.

Money

Now is the time to start saving for the future.

Work

We will achieve what we set out to do through self-discipline, determination and a structured way of thinking.

Andrew Laycock

The Hierophant

Two men stand before the Hierophant. They are waiting to be initiated into the society he represents, but first, they must unlock the mysteries of the universe to prove that they are worthy. They listen carefully to the Hierophant speak, for they know he has the answers they seek.

This card reminds us that the universe has the answers to all of the questions. If only we take the time to listen to what the universe is telling us. The Hierophant, meaning in Greek, the High Priest, is a kind and generous teacher we can turn to in times of trouble. But we have to be prepared to listen to his advice and accept his terms. There are no quick wins or gains to be had through cutting corners or following evil ways. Instead, when we turn this card, we must accept that traditional values and patience will be rewarded on the road ahead.

The Hierophant represents education and knowledge. When we turn this card, it suggests that we are being taught a lesson and have much to learn at this moment in time. What is it that we need to know? This is a time for contemplation, to spend some time in quiet thought to think through how we have got to this point in time and what we need to do to move forward. The Hierophant will help us, but only if we stick to the rules of life.

Sometimes we have the answers. At other times, we may need to talk through our situation with a trusted friend or mentor. If we are willing to search for the answer, the universe will help us, and if we need advice, we will find that the person who holds the key will enter our life. This could be someone completely new or someone we have known before. If we close our minds, however, and instead of searching for the answer, look for someone or something to blame, then nothing will change.

Love

The Hierophant guards against passion and lust. It is love and friendship that survives the test of time.

The Secrets Of The Tarot

Money

We need to think carefully about what we have done that has brought us to this financial situation. Only when we know how we have gotten to where we are now can we confidently move forward.

Work

We may be battling against restrictions imposed by others. We should pause before moving on, for they may provide a lesson that we need to learn

The Lovers

A common misconception with this card is that it is only about love. Even though a man and woman are depicted on the card who we believe are lovers, this is not the only message that the card has for us. In common with all cards in the tarot deck, it holds many secrets and answers, and if we focus solely on the message of love contained within the card, we can miss out or ignore the true meaning of the card.

The Lovers is a card about choice. When we draw this card, it often means that we have a decision to make. The choices we face need to be carefully analysed and thought through as they are likely to have a long-term impact on our future success and happiness. This card tells us that there are always two factors at play in any decision, two paths that we can take, two sides to the story. We can listen to our heart or listen to our head. We can listen to our inner voice or take advice from others. We can think only of ourselves, or we can think about how the decision affects those around us.

Although we are ultimately responsible for any decision we make in life, the card serves as a reminder that we are not alone in the world. Even if we think we are at this moment in time. Just as we are walking down our path in life, others are each taking their paths, and we need to be mindful not only of our needs but the needs of others and of what they may have that can help us on our journey. The card is a positive card to draw in that it reminds us that we are one person of many in the world. Still, it does warn us that individuals can be selfish and self-absorbed, either intentionally or unintentionally. If we think only of ourselves, we can risk alienating those around us. That is not to say that we should place a higher value on someone else's needs above our own, rather we should consider the needs of others as well as our own.

Love

The Lovers remind us that for a relationship to work, both people need the space to grow as individuals and respect each other's differences and needs.

Money

This card suggests financial growth is about to happen, but we should not be afraid to ask for help if it is coming slower than we need.

Work

Now is the time for us to make a choice. We can take advice from others, but only we know what we need to do.

Andrew Laycock

The Chariot

The soldier is directing his chariot into battle. His armour will protect him from the worst any challenger can throw his way. Although he needs to take the lead and drive the chariot forward, he is not alone. Supporting him in his quest are his trusted and reliable friends who will help him and take the strain when he needs them the most.

This card is about movement and driving forward towards our goals and aims. When drawn, it serves as a timely reminder that although the road ahead may be rocky and sometimes feels as though it is strewn with obstacles, we do not need to be alone on the journey. The past, and the knowledge and experience we have picked up on our journey so far, can help us if we are prepared to learn the lessons we have been taught. If it is worth it, no achievement can be attained without some effort on our part. In times of challenge, we must focus on our aim, stay disciplined and take control of whatever situations we face. We should not be afraid to call upon those friends and trusted advisors when we feel we need motivation or a friendly ear.

At times of change in our life, whether we are the instigators of the change or the changes have happened to us, this card tells us that through self-belief we can gain the confidence we need to take charge and direct events in our favour. The card reminds us to stay firm in the face of adversity and not allow anything or anyone to derail us. It does, however, provide us with the warning that there are always two routes to any destination, and we should take the one that holds us true to our values. The most accessible road may not always be the one that provides us with the most enjoyment or the lessons that we may need on the journey further ahead.

Love

In love, there are always two sides to consider, but we should stay true to our values and our heart.

The Secrets Of The Tarot

Money

There may be financial obstacles ahead. Now is not the time to spend but to conserve what we have, for we may need it to fight future battles.

Work

There are likely to be changes ahead that may be challenging. If we stay strong, focused, and disciplined, we will ultimately achieve success.

Strength

This card signifies the quiet strength that we all have within ourselves. The gentle woman and the forceful lion are at peace, content to be in each other's company. Neither needs to dominate or overcome the other. Competition is not required. There is no need for a winner and a loser. We can all gain what we want without the need to override the needs of others.

When we draw this card, we need to look to work with others, promote teamwork and harmony, search for common ground, and strive to achieve balance in whatever we aim to do. The card reminds us that it is not the person who has the most incredible physical strength, the loudest voice, or the biggest personality that necessarily achieves their aim. Often it can be the person who can work with others, inspire confidence, and lead without seeming to direct that can accomplish the most and do what needs to be done.

If we are to succeed in our aim, we should have courage, determination, and not be afraid to take the less travelled road, even though others may think we are foolish. It takes a brave person to face a lion and kill him, but an even braver one to take on a lion and tame him. In the same way, it is easy to tell others what to do and lead them into battle, but it is much harder to ask for their trust and get them to follow you. Now is the time for you to put others at the heart of what you do. You will achieve much more and gain much greater satisfaction if you focus on what others can do for you and equally what you can do for them.

The Strength card is a collaboration card. It is important that you do not lose sight of what you want to achieve, but equally important that you understand what others need from you. The lion can be tamed but should never be used solely for your purposes. If you use others without giving anything in return, they can soon become your enemy. Remember, if the lion becomes your enemy, it is he who has the greatest physical strength and can inflict the greatest harm.

Love

We should give love freely but not allow ourselves to be taken advantage of, nor take advantage of others. We all deserve the same from a partner as we give.

Money

Happiness comes from sharing what we have with others, but only if we have sufficient to meet our basic needs. If there are currently too many demands on our finances, we need to think carefully about where we can gain the greatest return.

Work

We should not strive for our goals at the expense of others. Collaboration and teamwork are the keys that will open the doors to further advancement in our careers.

Andrew Laycock

The Hermit

The Hermit stands quietly on the path, waiting for the message that he knows will come to tell him where he needs to go now. He has no sense of where the road will take him, or of what he will encounter on his travels, but trusts that the lamp in his hand will light his path and his cloak, though ragged, will keep him warm. It is all he has brought from his past life and all that he feels he needs. He stands and waits; there is no rush. The message will come when the time is right.

When we draw the Hermit, the Universe is giving us a clear message that before we go any further down the path that we are taking, we should take the time to stop and reassess where we have come from and identify where we need to go from here. This could mean that we need to temporarily take ourselves away from our current situation to have the time and the space to think clearly, unencumbered by the needs of others or our responsibilities. The Hermit shows us, above all else, that sometimes it is only by removing ourselves physically or mentally from our current state that we can find the answers we are looking for.

We were all put on this earth with a purpose, but often life gets in the way. We find ourselves going with the flow, doing what is expected of us, taking on roles through circumstances that we have had little control over. Now is the time to concentrate on what we want to do, regardless of the needs of others. That is not to say that we should be selfish and think only of ourselves, but instead that we should put ourselves first for once. To take time for ourselves, even if it is just a few minutes of quiet reflection, is a gift that we all deserve. And when we accept this gift, we will often be given a message that shows us the actions we need to take going forward. To bring ourselves greater happiness and contentment and by association improve the pleasure of those whose lives we touch.

The positive message in this card is clear: before proceeding, we need to stop, wait and value only time. Not allow ourselves to be weighed down by material objects or the responsibilities of others. However, there is a danger that we are so used to moving forward down a particular path that we forget to open our minds to other possibilities and only ask the Universe for reassurance that we are on the right track.

Love

We should think long and hard before committing ourselves.

Money

We may feel financial loss, but sometimes it is only when we think we have nothing that we can truly appreciate the value of life.

Work

Now is the time to assess whether we are doing what we were put on this earth to do.

The Wheel of Fortune

The Wheel of Fortune is a card about luck and chance. Luck can be both good and bad, but when we turn this card in a reading, it suggests that we will get a break, that luck and good fortune are going to be on our side. It reminds us, however, that all life is down to chance, and that what we will receive may not be quite what we expected or initially wanted.

When asking the tarot a question, we often look for a precise answer. We have something in mind that we want help and support with. We may, for example, be considering changing jobs and are consulting the tarot to see what guidance it can offer. In drawing the Wheel of Fortune, this card can signify that we need to do nothing, that luck is on our side, that a new opportunity will present itself. There is a rub, though, when we receive this card, and that is that the opportunity is likely to not at all be what we expected. It may be that we get offered a promotion in our current job or are given redundancy, which allows us to do something new. Our husband or wife may receive a new opportunity that means we have to relocate and start again somewhere else. This card may indicate good fortune at this moment, but it tells us to expect the unexpected and not to focus on one course of action and exclude all others.

This card is a very positive card for the present, for it signifies that in the here and now, or indeed the short term, we will be the recipient of good fortune. The card reminds us, though, that as quickly as we can be the recipient of good luck now, we can be the recipient of bad luck in the future. It tells us to make the most of the opportunities offered and not blame life when things go wrong. The wheel of fortune never stops turning, and nothing is or should be forever.

Love

Your circumstances are likely to change unexpectedly for the better.

Money

Financial good fortune is indicated, though it may not be what we were expecting.

Work

Do not get stuck on a specific course of action. Greater success is likely to come through progress and change, not through doing what has always been done

Justice

The Justice card represents balance, fairness, honesty and moderation. The Judge sits in her chair, holding in her left hand the scales of justice and in her right the sword of victory. Her message is clear. In life, we are responsible for our actions, and those actions have consequences. Success can be ours if we live a fair and truthful life. If we don't, if we seek to succeed at the expense of others, then we can only blame ourselves if justice of a different kind is dispensed in our direction.

We often find ourselves drawing the Justice card when a decision is to be made. A decision that can take us in two completely different directions. Although the card cannot provide us with the answer, or suggest one direction over another, it reminds us of how we should approach the decision. It tells us that there is a need for balance and order in our life, that we should weigh up the pros and cons of each decision carefully and rationally, and that we should reflect carefully before acting. Above all, it shows us that in making the decision, we should do what feels right not only to ourselves but also to those around us who may be impacted by any decision we make.

On a mundane level, the card can signify legal matters, signing contracts or papers, or a dispute or a complaint. How the legal issue will play out depends entirely on any other cards that have been drawn in the reading. Still, if we have acted reasonably and with integrity, it suggests that the legal matter is not something of which we should be afraid. The warning in the card, of course, is that what is fair to one person may not necessarily feel acceptable to another, and the card asks us to look at ourselves to ensure that we have acted in the best interests of others and ourselves. If we haven't, we should own up to our mistakes and make amends accordingly before matters are allowed to get out of hand.

Love

In love, this card signifies that we will get what we deserve. This could, of course, be good or bad!

The Secrets Of The Tarot

Money

Now is the time to put our finances in order.

Work

Contractual matters are highlighted, a possible new job or opportunity may come our way.

Andrew Laycock

The Hanged Man

A man is hanging upside down, suspended from a branch. On first looking at the card, he appears to have been placed there, maybe as a punishment for some misdemeanour. If we look closely, though, we can see that he has hung there himself, to take a break from the hustle and bustle of life, to pause and reflect on where he needs to go from here.

Often thought of as one of the most complex cards to read in the major arcana, it is actually one of the easiest. It tells us that we are at a junction on our journey through life, and we now need to pause whilst we consider what to do next. Although we don't need to hang ourselves upside down, we need to consider the next stage of our journey from a different perspective; otherwise, the card tells us that the next step in life will be just like the one that has gone before.

If we have had a happy life filled with successes and achievements, we may want to repeat the journey, but we need to be careful because life moves forward down a path, not around a wheel. We will not repeat the successes of a previous journey by looking at the new journey through the same pair of eyes. Similarly, if we have had a journey that we would rather forget, starting the next stage with the same views and ideas could lead us to make the same mistakes again. Now is our chance to stop and look at things differently, decide to make changes, and try something new.

This card hints at opportunities and reminds us that we may need to make sacrifices or adjustments that we may not find easy. We may need to let go of something that has provided us with great comfort on our last journey but may hinder us on the next. How long we pause here is up to us, for the card does not seek to rush us. Eventually, though, we will have to move. The card reminds us that as we move through the different phases of our lives, our view, like the hanged man, must change if we look forward and not back.

Love

The card suggests that we should look at love and relationships differently than we have before.

Money

Fortune favours the brave, but only if all the risks have been assessed.

Work

The Hanged Man signifies a new approach, but not a rash decision.

Death

The Death card is probably the most feared card in the tarot deck, and it is undoubtedly the one that is the most misunderstood. When people draw the death card, they often think it means death, either their own or someone close to them. It is important to remember, though, that nothing is quite what it seems in the tarot.

The Death card is one of the most beautiful cards in the tarot because it means the birth of something new, fresh and pure. Look closely at the card again if you have a deck to hand. The horse is white, signifying all that is pure. Death himself, represented as a skeleton, the part of our body that survives when we die, is clothed in protective armour, giving protection. The sun is in the background shining brightly on the dawn of a new day, and in the foreground, the clergyman bows low out of respect for the journey Death has completed to bring him here to this place.

The card demonstrates all that is positive about the death of one situation and the phase we are about to go through at the start of something new. At certain stages in our life, we all need to transform ourselves as we move from one period to the next. If the Hanged Man shows us that we need to pause and alter our perspective if we are to transition from one phase to the next, then the Death card means now is a time for celebration as the decision to change has been made and we can start afresh.

Death shows us that we are about to start something new, that the past is in the past and cannot be relived. Whatever the change is, whether it be the death of our single status and a new relationship, a move from one home to another, a new job, a change of attitude, the birth of a child, then we must accept that we are now a different person than the one we were before. We cannot cling to what we had out of comfort or nervousness. We now need to embrace the change and move forward.

Whether we want to change or not, we have to accept that we have. There is now no going back.

Love

In love, one set of circumstances has been replaced by something new.

Money

Our financial situation has changed. We need to adapt and not treat money the same as we have before

Work

The Death card signifies a change in career, a new business venture, or a job change.

Temperance

Temperance is a winged angel, but it is unclear on first looking at the card whether the angel is a man or a woman, which is deliberate because it represents balance. Balance is needed on earth and in life. The angel stands one foot on dry land, one foot in the water, reminding us that the very essence of this planet's being is because of the balance of the elements. S/he pours water from one cup to the other, trying to balance them so that neither cup gets more than the other, that the water, whether it is a blessing or a burden, is shared equally among the two cups. On one side of the angel, the land is dry and barren. On the other crops grow in plentiful supply. The natural world is full of opposites. When it is winter here, it is summer elsewhere, where there is peace in our home, there is noise outside our door, as someone dies, so someone else is born. It is the way of the world to be filled with opposites, just as in our life we will have days of great pleasure and times of despair.

    This card signifies that if we are to succeed in life or the task at hand, we need to strive for balance and harmony in everything we do. Just as we have needs and desires, then those close to us or around us do as well, and we should be mindful of what they want as much as what we want. That is not to say that we should put their needs higher than ours. Instead that we should look for solutions that both parties can accept. This is a card about compromise, being diplomatic, and accepting that there are others in this life we need on our side if we are to have a fulfilling life.

    Temperance reminds us that we are not alone in this world. Depending on our situation, we should either look to help those weaker than ourselves or seek help from those who are stronger. It is a card about sharing and giving, and as the cycle of life turns, sometimes we require assistance, and at other times we are in a position to provide it. We should never shy away from helping those in need, nor should we be too proud to ask for help if we need it.

Love

Opposites do attract, but we need to look for common ground if the relationship is sustained.

Money

There are demands on our finances, but we should try not to spend more than we earn.

Work

We may need to compromise on our plans and temper our ideas, but success can be achieved through discussion and the exchange of ideas.

Andrew Laycock

The Devil

At first sight, the Devil card depicts a man and a woman, naked and exposed, chained to a frightening mythical creature, half-man and half-beast. However, if we look closely, we can see that the chains are only loosely draped around the couple's neck. If they are captive, then it is because they wish to be so. If they wanted to, they could quickly release themselves.

It is often easier to allow ourselves to be controlled by a situation because then we can pass the responsibilities or the blame to someone or something else when we don›t get what we want. How often have you heard someone say, «I can›t do this because» or «It›s always been done this way» or even «that always happens to me»? Sometimes it is safer not to try something different and continue to do what we have always done, rather than put ourselves out there and try something new. If we take the initiative and try something new and it doesn›t work, we have to blame ourselves.

This card offers a warning that if we allow ourselves to be enslaved and dominated by a situation or a set of circumstances, we may not be truly fulfilled. Sure, we are not likely to put ourselves at risk, the card does not promise or indicate that if we try something new or different, we will succeed, but as the adage goes, it is sometimes better to try and fail than never to have tried at all.

Life is not always pleasant or rewarding. It can throw up challenges that we need to overcome. When this happens, it sometimes feels safer to retreat and pass the responsibility on to someone else, but if we do, we cannot learn the lessons that we may need further down the path. We may find ourselves repeating the same old actions over and over again, existing but not living. This card suggests that we should free ourselves from what may be holding us back and at least give something a go. But only if we can accept the consequences, whatever they may be.

Love

Are our fears and insecurities preventing us from getting what we truly want out of a relationship?

Money

The devil warns against taking comfort in material possessions, for they cannot love us back.

Work

This card suggests that we are chained by our responsibilities and asks us to question whether we are truly doing what we were meant to do.

Andrew Laycock

The Tower

Possibly the most visually dramatic of all the major arcana cards, a lightning bolt strikes a tower causing it to burst into flames. People fall headfirst from the window as it is destroyed, their arms flailing as they plunge into the unknown. The card doesn't just hint at destruction but screams a warning at us, telling us that the security we have known is about to be destroyed.

We may be forgiven for thinking that the Tower is a negative card, that it warns of impending doom, but this is not necessarily so. It depends, of course, on our attitude to change and whether or not we feel we need to change at this moment in our life. The Tower holds a warning that something unexpected is about to happen, that it will happen suddenly and without notice, that we are unlikely to have any control over it and that it will disrupt our plans. What we have known will collapse. But maybe this is needed if we are to move forward and progress.

Often, we take comfort in what we have known, but what we think of as safe and secure can keep us prisoner and hold us back. We don't look for a new job with more money because we like the people we work with and are scared of being the new person who knows nobody. We stay with our partner, with who we have nothing in common, because we are afraid of being on our own. We continue to blame the world for our troubles because we might have to admit that the problems are down to us if we don't. We find it easier to get by day by day with the same old activities and habits because trying something new may make things worse and not better. We may need to change to live the life that the Universe intended for us, but we don't want to. The Tower is life's way of giving us the kick we need, telling us that if we are not going to change ourselves, it will make it happen.

The Tower may cause us problems in the short term. What will happen may be unpleasant, but the Universe will not take everything. We will always have hope. We have been freed from what has been holding us back, and we can rebuild something new and better. That is the message we should always keep in our minds.

The Secrets Of The Tarot

Love

What we least expect to happen will happen, but it could be for the best.

Money

We should be prepared for a financial shock, a loss of income, or possibly an unexpected windfall.

Work

Change will happen when we least expect it.

The Star

A woman kneels on the earth, pouring water from a jug to replenish the pool in front of her. In her other hand, she holds a second jug, and the water flows from this onto the earth. Above her head are eight stars, one shining much brighter than the others. When she has finished her task, it is this one that she must follow if she is to reach the destination that she seeks.

    Coming as it does after the Tower, this card reminds us of new life. As the star in the night sky told the shepherds of the birth of Jesus Christ, the Star card tells us that we are at the start of a new journey. However, it offers a warning that if we are to reach our intended destination, we must not let anything distract us from our goals. Just as the woman in the card is unaware that water is spilling from the jug behind her, we are told that if we do not focus on the brightest star and instead allow the other stars to lead us astray, then we may not gain what we truly seek.

    Let us not focus too much on the negative aspect of this card, though, because the Star card is a card of faith and hope. The star that we should follow is bright and easy to see, and there is no reason to think that the other stars will outshine it. Unlike the Fool, who at the beginning of his journey is unsure where he wants to go, we know at this point in our journey through life where we need to go next. The Universe will light the way for us. Though the next stage of our journey will be easier than the one that has just passed, it will not be quick. Stars take many light years to light up the earth, and although it will not take us quite this long to achieve what we want, there will be no quick wins. Remember that anything worth having is worth waiting for if it is to be truly enjoyed.

Love

    Now is the time to focus on a new us. Maybe treat ourselves to a new hairstyle, a change of appearance, or a pamper day at the spa.

The Secrets Of The Tarot

Money

Money will flow in, but we need to be careful not to let it flow out just as quickly. Money is to be enjoyed and not to be wasted.

Work

We are going to get the recognition we deserve.

The Moon

The dog and the wolf stare expectantly at the moon, hoping it will light the way forward. Are they comrades on the journey, or have they just found themselves at the same place at the same time? It is clear that the path stretches far into the distance and that some stages will be easier than others, that they will need to conserve their energy on these parts so that they have the stamina to navigate the rugged terrain. They do not know what they will encounter on the journey and, therefore, what they will need. If they travel together, they may have companionship and support, but equally, they may turn against each other if the journey gets hard. It may be safer, of course, to travel independently, in which case they may not have the burdens of the other to carry, but then they cannot rely on the other for help if this is needed. They have much to think about, more than they realise, for looking only forward, they are unaware of what is behind them.

The moon is a complex card, for it represents what is unknown and offers more questions than answers. When we draw the Moon in a reading, it tells us that all is not as it seems. Appearances can be deceptive, and there is more to the decision that we have to make than meets the eye. It reminds us that although it is essential to focus on long term plans, it is just as important to consider what is needed in the here and now, for it is at this moment that we can start to build the foundations for any future success. The Moon warns us that even though we must prepare adequately for the journey ahead, we must ensure we have what we need now. If we don't, we may not start the journey, never mind complete it.

Like all cards in the tarot, the Moon highlights what we need to be successful whilst warning us of the dangers that can lead to our downfall. In this respect, the moon's message is clear. Now is the time to re-evaluate what we want in the future. What we want may not be what we need right now. This is the time to look around us and identify what provides help and support and what hinders us or holds us back. Now is not the time to trust but to question.

The Secrets Of The Tarot

Love

There may be a decision to consider. What we want over what we think we want. The card asks us to question our instincts before we trust them.

Money

There is no point saving for tomorrow if we cannot live for today.

Work

All may not be as it seems. Those that provide advice and guidance may have their best interests at heart, not ours.

The Sun

The Sun is the card of optimism and freedom. It reminds us that in the same way that the sun is the source of all growth on earth, then our self-belief and positive thoughts will help us achieve whatever we set out to achieve. Children do not stop and think of what may go wrong. The sunflowers in the field do not conserve their energy, hoping their lifespan will be longer. A child explores, sunflowers reach for the sun. This card asks us to reach for our dreams without worrying about what may go wrong. It asks us once again to have the belief and optimism of a child.

When we draw this card, it tells us now is the time to aim high and go for our dreams. It asks us to believe that we were put on this earth for a specific purpose, tells us that we should not waste our life existing but living. It shows us that to truly get the most out of life, we should not think about what may go wrong. It is not the time to focus on what we feel we cannot do, the challenges we face, the obstacles we think are in our way. Now is the time to go for it, embrace our dreams and stretch ourselves. When a child tries to walk, he does not believe that he is going to fall. When a baby screams, he trusts that his parents will come. When a child is asked what they want to be when they grow up, they tell you they want to be an astronaut, or a doctor, a footballer or a dancer. They have not yet learned to limit their beliefs. It is only when they grow up that they focus on the risks, challenges, and doubts. This card asks us to remember how free, optimistic, and confident we felt as children and go back to that state.

Love

Accept our partner or friend for who they are, do not try and change them for they are who they want to be

Money

We should illuminate our life with positive thoughts and manifest what we want in our life. We may be surprised at how the Universe responds.

Work

This card asks us to believe that we can be what we truly want to be. Now is the time to go for that promotion, start that new venture, apply for a role in a company where we have always wanted to work. It is a risk, but if it doesn't work out, then at least we have tried.

Judgement

They rise from their coffins, arms outstretched in joy, responding to the trumpet call of the angel hovering above them. They have been woken from the dead and are ready to live again.

The Judgement card is all about communication. This card indicates that it is time to tell the world the journey we have been on, the changes we have made, and where we are heading. Why is this important, we may ask ourselves? It is our journey, personal to us, and those closest to us should see the differences or know what we want to do. This may be true, but people often do not see change unless we tell them. What is obvious to us may not be evident to others. If we have changed inside, then the final step is to announce to the world that we have changed. If we have decided to do something new with our life, now is the time to share our plans with those around us.

Just as we are sharing our news with others so that they can recognise that a new being has replaced the old us, so we will ourselves start to feel differently. We can let go of the past, we have learned from the actions we have taken or the mistakes we have made, we can release ourselves from the confines of our thoughts that kept us trapped and unable to move forward. We can now feel that nothing is holding us back, that the weight of the past has been lifted from our shoulders, and we can move into a brighter, lighter future. We do not know at this stage what awaits us in the next life, but we should go forward bravely and not be afraid to tell people where we are going.

In common with all cards, the Judgement card offers a warning. As the people rise from their coffins naked, ready to live again, the card warns us not to take with us the burdens of our past journey. We do not need them. We will pick up what we need on our way there.

The Secrets Of The Tarot

Love

We recognise how to handle our relationships. We do not need to sacrifice our happiness for someone else's. We do not need to feel guilty for our actions. It is a chance to start afresh.

Money

The Judgement card reminds us that material possessions can be both a burden and a joy. The most valuable commodity in life comes not through what we have but how we live.

Work

Now is the time to share with people what we want to do next, for they may not know unless we tell them.

The World

Imagine that the woman depicted on the card is trapped inside the wreath. The wreath will soon open, allowing her to move outside, where four very different opportunities await her. At this moment, she can only dream of these opportunities, they are beyond her grasp, and because they are only vague thoughts, she has no idea which one she will choose. She needs to think some more and look back on the lessons she has learned. In time all will become clear.

The World is the last of the major arcana cards. It is the completion of our journey of self-knowledge, but it reminds us that in life, the cycle does not end. As one cycle completes its turn, so another one starts. Soon we will be able to begin a new journey confident that we have the skills and knowledge that we need to go forward successfully. That is for another day. The Universe wants us to pause, rest, and enjoy what we have before starting something new.

The World is always a positive card in a reading because it signifies that we have achieved what we were meant to do in the cycle of our life that has just been completed. That stage is over now, and we can take some time to enjoy what we have. Before we transition to the next phase of our life, it is essential to wait, replenish our energies, and take some time to live in the moment. We need to be careful that we do not think we have everything we want; there is a difference between taking some time to enjoy what we have achieved and becoming trapped in our old life and not moving on. Although now is the time to celebrate our accomplishments and achievements, it will soon be time to turn our eyes towards new horizons and think about what else we can do.

Often, we turn this card just as we are on the cusp of a new phase in our life, moving from being single to being in a relationship, changing jobs, taking retirement, travelling to a new country for work, moving house. It reminds us that we can go forward with confidence because we have learned the lessons that will help us, but we should not rush in. The message above all others in this card is to live in this moment and enjoy what we have now.

Love

If we open our hearts, the way forward becomes clear.

Money

There are so many choices in this world and so many demands on our money. This card asks us to think carefully about how we spend our money and find the balance between spending on what we need, buying what we want and saving for tomorrow.

Work

Soon doors that we felt were closed will open up to us, but now is the time to wait. There is no need for us to try and force our way through.

We have now finished our journey through the major arcana. Before we go, let us remind ourselves what each of the cards and the people we have met tell us, for they all have a story to tell and a message to share:

The Fool tells us that to progress on the path ahead, we should know where we want to go.

The Magician reminds us that we have the skills and knowledge to succeed, if only we learn how to use them.

The High Priestess shares with us the knowledge that sometimes we should trust our instinct and intuition and not look too deeply for an answer to our situation.

The Empress reminds us to value what we have now, to take pleasure in the moment and enjoy the simple things in life.

The Emperor tells us that to go forward successfully, we need to have strong foundations in place, a plan of action and a systematic approach.

The Hierophant wants us to listen to what the Universe is telling us. When we meet him, it suggests that we have a lesson to learn.

The Lovers show us that there are always two factors at play in any situation. When we have a choice to make, we should weigh up each factor carefully to ensure we make the right one.

The Chariot is there to demonstrate that sometimes we need to drive forward boldly towards our goals and aims, show great determination and be forceful.

The Strength card reminds us that sometimes a much gentler approach is needed, that outstanding achievements can be made through working harmoniously with others.

The Hermit tells us that it is important to take ourselves away from a situation to have the time and the peace to make a decision.

The Wheel of Fortune shows us that life is often about chance. When we get a break, we should not question why but seize it with both hands.

Justice is a card about fairness, honesty and moderation. The judge asks us to think carefully about any decision and do what is right.

The Hanged Man suggests that now may be the time to pause and get a different perspective on a situation.

Death reminds us to take pleasure in the birth of something new.

Temperance asks us to consider the feelings and needs of others in any decisions that we are to make.

The Devil, on the other hand, tells us not to be so constrained by the needs, wants and desires of others that we end up being controlled by them.

The Tower provides us with a shock, for sometimes in life, that is precisely what we need.

The Star reminds us to follow our dreams and not let distractions get in our way.

The Secrets Of The Tarot

The Moon tells us that all may not be what it seems.

The Sun tells us to believe in ourselves and throw caution to the wind.

Judgement reassures us that we have nearly completed what we have set out to do, and now is the time to tell the world.

The World asks us to enjoy this moment but not become complacent. We have reached the end of this journey, but another one is about to start. If only we dare to push once more ahead.

Andrew Laycock

The Cups of Consciousness

Depending on the deck we are using, cups can also be called bowls, chalices, coupes, goblets and vases. They focus on the journey we make to bring our feelings to fruition. The cups take us from the unconscious feelings we have when we sense we want something, to recognising and consciously bringing those feelings into our thoughts, turning those thoughts into words, and finally taking action to manifest those feelings so we achieve our hearts desire. If we follow the messages in the cups, we think what we feel, say what we believe, and do what we say. That, in a nutshell, is the story of the Cups of Consciousness.

The suit of cups has fourteen cards, an ace, or the first card, through all the numbers to ten and then four court cards, Page, Knight, Queen and King. The numbered cards tell the story from unconsciousness through consciousness to action, and the court cards give further insight into the emotions we feel at each stage. Let us now look at what guidance the Cups of Consciousness can provide us with when they appear in a reading.

Ace of Cups

"My cup runneth over" is a phrase that immediately comes to mind when I see the Ace of Cups in a reading, and it is certainly apt when we consider the meaning of this card. In the Bible, which is where the phrase originates, it means that God provides not only what we need but more than we need. This is the key message that should be taken when we see this card. The cup overflows with water, signifying our emotions' movement from a state of unconsciousness to consciousness. We are starting the journey to put our vague feelings into something that we can visualise. If we believe and trust in the power of our thoughts, then we will be rewarded and receive from the Universe more than we ever thought possible.

When we see the Ace of Cups, it is a sign that we are starting on the path towards true fulfilment, where we will receive everything we want from life. It asks us not only to believe in our intuition but also to develop it, not waste time asking questions as to why we feel how we do, but to listen to what the Universe is telling us. If we want to start a creative project, now is the time to do it. If we have dreamed of taking up a new hobby, we should take the first steps. If we are looking for love, now we can find it. We will receive more than we imagine if only we trust ourselves to make a start.

There is, of course, another message in the card that is brought to us by the dove. The dove flies above the cup to drop a small disc into the centre. The dove symbolises peace and love, and on a mundane level, the Ace of Cups is a card of love. The Universe is bringing us the gift of love. If we are single, we may find love. If we are in a relationship, we may renew our love and commitment to each other. From passion to friendship and everything in between, this card highlights that we have abundant love coming into our lives.

Love

Love is high on the agenda at this time.

Money

We may receive a gift that will help us start a new project or follow a dream.

Work

Now is the time to start a creative project or turn our ideas into action.

Two of Cups

A man and a woman face each other as they exchange cups, watched over by a winged lion. This is a card with a dual message, demonstrating not only harmony, trust and unity but also that at this time, the flames of passion are intense. We should not assume that this card is solely about love because, in life, we can be passionate about many things. The driving forward of an idea or belief. The desire to possess an item or make changes in our lives that we feel are much needed or long overdue.

When we see the two of cups, we are reminded that two heads are often better than one in life. We may be coming to realise that to succeed in our endeavours, to take our thoughts and dreams forward, to put them into a plan of action, or to make a decision as to what we need to do next, we need a second opinion or the help and support of a willing or loving partner. The Universe is telling us that there are people who can help us achieve our hopes and our dreams, that we should not keep our thoughts hidden away but vocalise them, let them shine and seek out support where we can find it.

A mistake that we often make when looking for partners who can help us in life is to associate with people who share our same interests, opinions, and views. We believe they will bring the greatest benefit, but it is often a different view, an alternate perspective that can give us the flash of inspiration that gets the most significant rewards. We are asked when we see this card to broaden our horizons and minds, and open our hearts and our eyes to the limitless possibilities that the Universe provides.

Love

It may be time to look at things from a different perspective.

Money

Now is the time to look for an investor or supporter if a dream is to be realised.

Andrew Laycock

Work

This card suggests that a partnership will bring the most remarkable success.

Three of Cups

"It's my party, and I'll dance if I want to, dance if I want to, dance if I want to. You would dance too if it happened to you."

Ok, so the words of the well-known song are slightly different to these, but if there is one key message above all others in the suit of cups, it is that we should put a voice to our thoughts and words to our feelings. When I see the three of cups, these are the words that I feel. Three young women stand in a circle, their cups raised high above their heads in celebration and triumph. At their feet, the ground is covered in fruit and flowers, signifying the abundance that the natural earth provides. This card is a card of pure joy, beauty and the sweet smell of success. They are dancing with joy and celebrating what they have achieved.

It seems strange to many people that this card appears so early in our journey through the cups, for on the face of it, we have not achieved anything yet. Remember, though, that the suit of cups represents the flow of feelings from the unconscious state to the conscious state and, as we have now put a voice to our thoughts, have made them tangible and real there is much to celebrate. This card provides us with the message that if we follow our hearts, we will begin to enter a period of happiness and fulfilment. If we let our thoughts grow, nurture them, and give them room to flourish, we will see our dreams manifest into everything we desire. It does ask us though, in common with the two of cups, not to keep our dreams to ourselves but to share them with others. That the greatest pleasure will be in sharing what we feel and as we share with others so we will ourselves gain support and friendship in return.

On a mundane level, this card signifies that we may be approaching a time where the greatest comfort and pleasure comes from our friends, family and co-workers. We should look for opportunities to network and meet in a social setting, share ideas, thoughts and generally have fun.

Love

We may meet someone who we are attracted to, or if we are in a relationship, we will have a reason to celebrate

Money

This is not a card of material wealth, but of finding riches in life of a different kind.

Work

We should take the time to socialise with colleagues, co-workers and business associates. All work and no play makes for a very dull working day.

Four of Cups

A young man sits under a tree, calm and seemingly at peace. He has arranged his cups in front of him in a neat line, and though they are in plain sight, he takes no notice of them, for he is lost in his thoughts. A hand appears from the air around him and offers him another cup but, lost as he is in his mind, he either does not see it or does not want it. Of course, we cannot tell which it is because we cannot ask him, and even if we could, he may not listen or acknowledge our existence, for he does not look very approachable. Perhaps he is not at peace after all, but instead, unhappy with his thoughts.

The symbolism in the four of cups card, in common with all the cards in the tarot, can be interpreted in many ways. When we sit with our arms crossed across our chest like the man sitting under the tree, it can mean we are comfortable, resting, and at peace with ourselves. On the other hand, it could mean that we are being defensive, unhappy, and protecting ourselves from those around us. When faced with this card, we will only know the emotions we feel in the context of the question we are asking, or can see the other cards in the reading. Rather than focus on what we don't know, let us look at what we do know when we see this card.

This card appears when we have got our thoughts in order and have decided what we will do to move forward. Before we start the journey, it is time for us to sit quietly and think things through, check if we have considered all the options, and review our plans to see if they will help us reach our goals. It is a time for contemplation, not progress, the calm before the storm of action. We have put our feelings into thoughts, and our thoughts into words, created plans and now need to pause awhile to identify if this is what we want or need to do to complete the journey successfully to what our heart desires.

The introduction of the fourth cup is, of course, bringing us another thought or idea and, with it, a warning. It reminds us that random thoughts can spring into our mind, unbidden but not necessarily unwanted, when we spend time in quiet contemplation. We haven't considered alternatives. It may be an opportunity that will help us achieve what we want quicker, with more fulfilment. The thought maybe something we should grab with both hands. It could, though, be a rogue thought, one that will distract us, take us off course. It may be something we need to discard quickly before it takes hold and plants a seed of doubt in our minds. Whether the thought is good or bad, the one thing we shouldn't do is ignore it, for we ignore it at our peril. We do not want the thought to fester at the edge of our consciousness until a later date.

Love

The card suggests that we will discover something about a lover or partner that we did not previously know.

Money

We will receive an unexpected bonus or expense.

Work

There may be a different approach to achieving a task or objective.

Five of Cups

A man stands on a path, his cloak wrapped tightly around him. Lying in front of him are three upturned cups, spilling their contents out into the ground to be soaked up by the hard earth, whilst two cups stand upright behind him. He does not notice what remains because his attention is drawn only to what he has lost.

On the face of it, this is a card of distress and despair. What we thought we could do, we have realised we can't. What we thought we had, we have now accepted we haven't. The card serves to remind us, though, that when things have not gone to plan, when goals have had to be abandoned, all does not need to be thrown away. We may not be able to do or have everything we wanted, but we can still rescue something from our thoughts and take this forward.

Our journey does not have to end when we hit a setback. If we drop an egg when baking a cake, we can continue to make a smaller cake with the remaining eggs we have left. If we take a wrong turn on our drive to the airport and miss the flight that we were going to take, we could always take another flight or go somewhere else for the weekend. The five of cups asks us to not hide away when things go wrong and waste time wallowing in self-pity, but instead turn our attention to what remains and take the opportunity to make something else. It may not be what we wanted or planned, but it can still be fulfilling and worthwhile.

Love

The five of cups reminds us that the path of true love never did run smooth.

Money

We may not have enough to do everything we had planned, but there is no need to do nothing. We should temper our ambitions at this time.

Andrew Laycock

Work

Our plans may need to change in the face of a setback, but we should not be inactive. We will get nowhere by standing on the sideline.

Six of Cups

Coming straight after the despair of the last card, the six of cups is a beautiful card filled with positive energy. It reminds us of childhood, of a time when we had no worries, a time of innocence when our present was filled with pleasure and fun, and our future held the promise that all our hopes and dreams would be fulfilled.

A young boy hands a cup filled with flowers to an even younger girl, and the card asks us to remember a time when we were happy to accept all the gifts the universe had for us without question. As adults, we often search for meaning for everything we receive. If we receive good fortune, we immediately think that something terrible will happen to even up the score. If someone offers us a gift, then we automatically assume that there must be a catch, that we will be expected to return the favour in the future. If we are lucky, we wonder what we have done to deserve it, for we believe that there must always be a reason for anything good that happens to us. Sometimes we need to remember how we felt as a child and accept without question the gifts that the universe has for us.

There is, of course, another meaning in the card, and this is that if we are currently experiencing good fortune and abundance in our life, we should look for opportunities to pay it forward. If we are on the path to our dreams and can put our thoughts and words into action, we should help others start on the journey themselves. Only we will know, when this card appears in the reading, whether we are in the position of the young girl receiving the gift or whether we are the boy who is in the position to give it. Whichever we are, this card reminds us that we should always give or accept readily and freely in life.

Love

On a mundane level, this card suggests that people from our past may return to our life.

Money

　Now could be the time to invest in someone else to allow them to grow, or it may be a time for us to ask for investment to help make our dreams a reality.

Work

　We should find people to collaborate with who have the same values and goals as ourselves.

Seven of Cups

We can all spend part of our time daydreaming, living a portion of our lives in Fantasyland. In some circumstances, it is an enjoyable place to be, somewhere we can spend a happy few minutes away from the pressures and problems of our own life. Sometimes it is somewhere that we need to be because it helps keep us safe and protects us from the difficulties of our situation. Occasionally though, it is dangerous, because it can lead us to lose sight of reality and draw us away from the actions we need to take to change our lives for the better.

In the seven of cups, we are reminded of the dangers of spending too long thinking and not enough time doing. Daydreaming has its place, but we must never forget that we inhabit the real world, and if we spend too long with our thoughts and dreams, then our mind can become so focused on the imaginary world that we forget to do anything with them. If we are to succeed in life, we need to turn our thoughts into action and make what we imagine a reality.

It would be a mistake, though, to think that this card only carries a warning because cards in the tarot deck are neither bad nor good. They have many messages contained within them. The positive with the seven of cups is that it suggests that there may be many opportunities heading our way, and we will be spoilt for choice. Not every opportunity will provide the same potential, though, so we will need to think carefully and analyse the pros and cons of each one. Thinking carefully does not mean spending so much time with our thoughts that we don't do anything with them or allow our minds to get cluttered. A decision will ultimately need to be made, and as this is the suit of cups, we should go with the one that our conscious mind tells us feels right.

Love

The reality of our situation could be very different from what we want. But then, do we know what we want?

Money

We are spending too much of our time thinking about money rather than making it.

Work

We have overstretched ourselves, given ourselves far too much to do, and retreated to a place where we are achieving nothing.

Eight of Cups

The Eight of Cups is another card that we can interpret differently depending on the situation we find ourselves in or the question we have asked. A man strides off into the distance, leaving his cups stacked neatly on the path behind him. As we know, cups represent our feelings, thoughts and dreams. When we look at this card, we may see a man who has got his ideas in order and is now acting to turn them into reality, or we could instead see someone who has decided the task ahead is too complex and is abandoning his dreams and leaving them behind. Which one feels right to us at this moment time?

Let us first think optimistically. After the jumble of thoughts we had in our heads in the last card, we have now finally managed to get them into a logical order and set ourselves a structured plan. We know what we need to do with our thoughts to turn them into reality, and so we decide to make a start before we change our minds. Time is of the essence. We do not want to wait, so we set off into the unknown. We know where we are heading, for we have a plan to act as our map on the journey ahead, but we don't know what we will encounter. We sense that there will probably be obstacles to navigate and climb, but we feel confident that we have the tools to deal with them. We have started our journey.

But what if we think the journey is too challenging? When we draw this card, we may feel that the way ahead has too many risks. Having got our thoughts in order, we become overwhelmed with what we need to do. It is too dangerous. There are too many unknowns. We turn our back on our dreams, leaving them in the recesses of our minds. They will never be anything more than dreams.

When we turn this card, it is the Universe's way of urging us to follow our dreams and put them into action. If we have doubts, if we look like we will leave them behind, the Universe asks us to reconsider. Just as the man setting off has the moon to light his way, a stick to keep him safe and a cloak to keep him comfortable, we also have what we need to succeed. We are nearly there. We have only a few more steps to take. We should not give in now.

Love

We should not turn our back on what we have.

Money

The card asks us not to risk all we have pursuing something new. Yes, we should speculate to accumulate, but not with everything we have.

Work

The skills, knowledge and experiences we have gained already will help us in the next phase of our journey.

Nine of Cups

"Sitting pretty" is a phrase that always comes to mind when I see this card. The man on the card has everything he needs. He is almost bursting with pride, filled with contentment, as he sits in front of the cups he has collected.

The cups represent the attainment of all his dreams, and he can now sit back and put them on display for the whole world to see. For him, the journey is complete, and we can all admire his achievements. Many tarot readers refer to this card as the wish card as it is the card that means that our wishes will be granted. When we see this card in a reading, the law of attraction works powerfully for us. Whatever we want, the Universe will provide, assuming, of course, that we keep our side of the bargain and put some effort in ourselves. Providing we have put our thoughts into action, then the Universe will help us achieve what we desire and receive everything we deserve.

There is a warning in the card, though. We can only sit back and do nothing when we have achieved our dreams. We cannot expect the Universe to provide with no effort on our part. A book will not write itself. A man will not fall at our feet. Money does not grow on trees. If we make an effort, then the Universe will help us, but it will not do the hard work for us. If we write a book, the Universe will help ensure that it is seen by a publisher who wants such a book. If we socialise, we will discover that an eligible man is in the same location. If we work hard, then we will be rewarded.

The man has attained his dreams and now can sit back and enjoy his life. For him, the hard work is over. For us, depending where on our journey we are, it may only just be starting. We cannot and should not expect the Universe to do all the work for us. If we do, we will have wasted our chance.

Love

Now is the time to tell the Universe exactly what we want.

Money

Our hard work will be rewarded.

Work

Our talents and skills will be recognised.

Ten of Cups

A couple stands together, their arms held aloft as they look towards a rainbow filled with cups in the sky. In the foreground, two children link arms and dance with joy, whilst in the background, we can see a small, freshly painted house in a lush green meadow by a stream. If the story told by the suit of cups is a fairy tale, then this would be the "and they all lived happily ever after" at the end of the book.

The rainbow of cups we see in the sky symbolises the end of life's hardships and the beginning of a time of abundance where, if we have followed the rainbow, and made the journey of consciousness, then we truly have found the pot of gold at the end. When the ten of cups appears in a reading, it signifies a time when all our hopes and dreams have come true. It is a time for rejoicing, for thanking the Universe for all it has provided to us and for taking the time to celebrate the accomplishments we have made. We have turned our dreams into reality and can now enjoy the life that we have made.

Love

We can take pleasure in our family and friends, secure in the knowledge that we can live happily ever after.

Money

We have sufficient money for our needs. We may not necessarily be rich, but we have enough for what we want to do.

Work

We are doing what we were meant to do. This is a time when work does not feel like work.

Andrew Laycock

The Page of Cups

The Page of Cups stands on firm and solid ground, the sea rising and falling behind him. He holds a cup from where leaps a fish, causing him much surprise. How did it get in there, and what should he do with it? For the moment, he does not know. He can only stand and stare.

When the Page of Cups appears in a reading, it is a sign that we will soon be presented with something out of the blue. We do not know at this stage whether it will be good or bad, a help or a hindrance, for it depends very much on the circumstances and the situation in which we find ourselves. If the Page were expecting the cup to be filled with refreshing water to quench his thirst, he would not want to find a fish. It means he would not be able to drink. If, however, he was hungry, then the fact that a fish has found its way into his cup with no effort on his part is a piece of good fortune that he would be stupid to ignore.

We are on a journey to put our feelings into thoughts, our thoughts into words and our words into action. Wherever we are on this journey, the Page tells us that we are about to receive something unexpected that should make us stop, pause for a moment and evaluate whatever this new something is. Whether we wanted it or not, the Universe has presented it with us for a reason, and it should be considered. It may take many forms, a new idea that comes to us when we think we know what we want out of life, an event that may take us slightly off the track that we were on, an opportunity that seems too good to ignore. Whether we feel it will help us or not, we should take the time to evaluate it in the context of our desires and then use or discard it as we see fit.

Love

Are we expecting too much from a person? We should value their qualities rather than expect them to have the qualities that we want them to have.

Money

We need to consider the value money has, for it is not how much we have but what we can do with it that matters.

Work

The work we are doing is not what we expected it to be, but this is not necessarily bad. However, we may want to consider whether we are happy doing what we are doing or if our talents lie elsewhere.

Andrew Laycock

Knight of Cups

The Knight of Cups rides in to view slowly, holding his cup in front of him as if it is a precious gift he must present to the most worthy soul. His horse is white, signifying strength and purity, and his helmet is winged, symbolising the power of creative thought.

When the Knight of Cups appears in a reading, he is there to bring us the message that we are now at the start of a fantastic journey. One that may well transform our lives forever. It is a beautiful card to draw, for it holds the promise of untold riches. Not necessarily in a material sense but in an emotional one. The cup the Knight is carrying so carefully, as with all cups, represents an idea, a thought or a dream. In the case of this card, it tells us that an idea we have had, or a thought that will soon come to us, is one that, if we treasure and nurture, will bring us everything we desire in life.

Before we get too carried away with excitement, the Knight of Cups in common with all cards does hold a warning. It is that we should not get so caught up in the fantasy of what our life is going to be like that we rush in and mess everything up in our eagerness to grab what the universe has in store. Now is a time for slow, deliberate steps, to take our time, to move forward calmly. We will attain success when the time is right.

On a mundane level, the Knight of Cups signifies that we may receive a message that brings the spark of an idea or a drop of magic. If we are thinking of changing jobs, we could get an email telling us that there may be redundancies, which will provide us with a pay-out that will help us invest in our own business. If we are trying to find love, we may get an invitation to a party, if we are looking for our dream house in the country, we may take a wrong turning and as we turn the car around, see a For Sale sign peeping out from behind a hedge. This card tells us to keep an eye out for the messages that the universe will provide, for they may lead us to our dreams.

The Secrets Of The Tarot

Love

We may have an idealised view of love and be in love with the idea of being in love.

Money

A new potential source of income may suddenly reveal itself to us.

Work

This card signifies that a new opportunity may come into view over the horizon.

Andrew Laycock

Queen of Cups

The Queen of Cups sits on her throne on a beach, her feet almost but not quite touching the water. She holds a beautiful gold cup in her hand, which she stares at with wonder, hardly daring to believe that she can possess something so wonderful. Her throne and clothes are richly decorated, she carries a crown on her head, she is surrounded by angels. To the outside world, she appears to have it all, but there is a sadness about her that we cannot immediately understand. If we look at the signs and symbolism in the card, though, we can begin to understand why.

Unlike the other cups shown in the cards in the tarot deck, the cup the Queen is holding is closed. She is unable to see what treasures it contains. Although angels surround her, one of them hides from her. She does not know what his intentions are. Her feet are almost but not quite touching the water. Everything the Queen wants and desires is close to hand, but she cannot take the final step to get what she wants.

When we see the Queen of Cups in a reading, it means that we are repressing our true feelings, questioning what we want, looking for a logical explanation for our dreams. We may have a well-paid job that we studied hard for, but it may provide us with no satisfaction and we don't know why. We could have a beautiful home, which gives us no comfort, or a marriage that for some reason no longer supplies us with the joy or security that it once did. The Queen is here to remind us that sometimes there is no logical and rational explanation for how we feel. Instead of looking into our heads for the answers, we now need to look within our hearts. If we do, then the answer will reveal itself in time.

It may be that we need help to unblock our emotions. On a mundane level, the Queen suggests that now may be an excellent time to see a psychic, counsellor or coach. We may need to look for someone who has the skills and experience to help us find the way through this current phase in our life and unlock the emotions within.

The Secrets Of The Tarot

Love

We are repressing our true feelings. Only when we unlock what is hidden deep within our hearts can we start to get what we want.

Money

The card reminds us to not waste money on material possessions that have no real value.

Work

What we want seems just beyond our reach, but if we are honest about what we want, we may find it easier to obtain.

Andrew Laycock

King of Cups

The King of Cups sits on his throne, adrift on a turbulent sea. Despite his predicament, he is composed, confident that the stone block on which his throne is placed will not capsize and tip him headlong into the water. His experience and wisdom tell him that he will be perfectly safe if he stays still and does not make sudden moves.

When the King of Cups appears in a reading, the Universe is telling us that now is a time to be calm and still even if we don't want to be. A maelstrom of thoughts are likely to be swirling around in our head, ideas we can develop, dreams we can expand upon, and options we can investigate. We feel like a child in a sweet shop wanting to touch and taste everything on offer to see which one holds the most promise, but the King is here to remind us that we need to wait. That if we try everything, we may end up with nothing. Suppose we rush in to try and develop every idea that we have. In that case, we could burn ourselves out in the attempt, going in several directions at once and ending up exactly where we started. Worse, we may end up tipping ourselves into a disaster where we sink under the weight of the burdens we have put ourselves under. Now is the time to take control of our thoughts and demonstrate discipline.

On a mundane level, the King of Cups may represent an experienced and wise person who may come into our lives and help us make sense of all the available options. It may be a man or a woman, an experienced lawyer, business adviser or mentor who can listen to our ideas and advise us of the best way to go.

Love

We should be satisfied with what we have and not do anything to rock the boat.

The Secrets Of The Tarot

Money

The King warns us against making any rash, spur of the moment decisions.

Work

Now is the time to take a disciplined approach to work tasks or decisions.

We have now completed our journey through the Cups of Consciousness. The story helps us turn our innermost feelings into thoughts, then words and finally into actions. They help us attain what our heart desires. Let us summarise what we have learnt from each of the cards.

The Ace of Cups gives us the gift of consciousness to start our journey.

The Two of Cups urges us to verbalise our feelings to someone else.

The Three of Cups celebrates our leap from unconscious feelings to conscious thoughts.

The Four of Cups shows us that we should not close our minds to other opportunities.

The Five of Cups tells us to focus on what we have gained, not lost.

The Six of Cups asks us not to question what we receive.

The Seven of Cups warns us not to get distracted by our thoughts.

The Eight of Cups reminds us that we have everything we need to turn our words into actions.

The Nine of Cups proves that we can achieve everything we wish for if we work hard.

The Ten of Cups shows us we can have the "happy ever after" if we follow our dreams.

The Page of Cups tells us to expect the unexpected.

The Knight of Cups brings us a gift from the Universe to help us on our way.

The Queen of Cups asks us to unlock our hearts so that we can receive what we truly want.

The King of Cups urges us to take control of our thoughts if we are to keep on the path and achieve what we desire.

The Prosperous Pentacles

The pentacles, the most common name for the gold discs depicted on the tarot cards of this suit, are also known occasionally as circles, coins, discs, shields and talismans. They represent our relationship with the material world through financial matters, business affairs, wealth and possessions. They are neither positive nor negative, and the guidance they give is often associated with our feelings around material wealth instead of predicting whether money is coming in or going out of our life.

The suit of pentacles has fourteen cards in total, an ace, or the first card, through all the numbers to ten and then four court cards, Page, Knight, Queen and King. The cards each give a different insight into our relationship with material wealth, money or possessions. As cards of the minor arcana, they highlight mundane matters instead of life-changing events. When we see a card in the pentacles suit, it is more likely to guide what we need to do daily rather than offer guidance on significant income or expenditure. Let us now look at what advice the Prosperous Pentacles can give us when they appear in a reading.

Andrew Laycock

Ace of Pentacles

All Aces represent the start of a journey. The Ace of Pentacles shows a hand emerging from a cloud proffering a large gold coin. When we turn this card in a reading, it signifies that we will receive an injection of cash into our life or an offer of material possessions of a different kind.

Thank goodness, you probably think, which is a common reaction when people receive the Ace of Pentacles. We always feel we could do with a little more, however much wealth we have. It is important, though, to understand that the pentacles, as well as representing prosperity, also have a close link to the grounding element, earth. Any new money coming our way is likely to be relatively modest. When we see this card, we should not aim for the sky with our spending plans, but keep our feet firmly on the ground.

That is not to say, though, that we won't feel the benefits of renewed prosperity in our life. Whether it is an increase in money from being promoted, a financial investment that suddenly starts doing better than before, or an unexpected windfall or legacy, then we will undoubtedly feel more confident about treating ourselves to a few little luxuries. This, in turn, can lead us to feel happier about ourselves and more optimistic about life. It may even lead us to think about taking more risks with money. This latter is where the warning in this card lies. Yes, we can indulge ourselves a little, but we should not squander away our good fortune because the Ace of Pentacles does not bring a limitless pot of gold. We should remember this and not waste what we have been given.

Love

Now would be an excellent time to pamper ourselves or treat ourselves to a luxury item we usually wouldn't buy.

Money

A one-off injection of cash is forecast, which may be something we have

The Secrets Of The Tarot

worked hard for or come entirely out of the blue.

Work

This card suggests a promotion or new job is on the horizon.

Andrew Laycock

Two of Pentacles

The Two of Pentacles is a card first, and foremost, about balance. In the picture on the card, we see a young man standing with his back to a turbulent sea, juggling two gold coins between a piece of rope. He must concentrate hard to keep them in the air because if he loses focus and lets one slip between his fingers, the other would surely follow. Such is his concentration on the task in hand that he cannot see that the up-and-down motion of his coins matches almost exactly the up-and-down movement of the sea. So often we find that life imitates art, or should it be the other way around?

When we see this card in a reading, it tells us that we are entering a time where we will need all our skills and experience to carefully balance our money to have enough for our needs and the commitments we have made. There are many demands on our finances, so we need to be very clever to utilise our money to its best advantage. There are times when we may need to adapt our plans, prioritise our goals, put off buying one item so that we have enough for another, but we should not worry because if we are careful, we will be fine. We should also look for ways to make money instead of relying on our current income routes. Is there junk in our attic that may become a treasured item in someone else's home? Perhaps those homemade greetings cards that we make for family and friends may be saleable to others?

There is also a broader meaning in the Two of Pentacles. As well as balancing our finances, we may need to balance our financial management with the other aspects of our life. We should not focus on money to exclude everything else, our home, our family, our health. If we do, we may find over time that although we are financially wealthy, our life itself may be poorer as a result.

Love

We need to balance our needs with the needs of those we love.

The Secrets Of The Tarot

Money

There may be choppy waters ahead as we try to balance our finances, but we will be fine if we are careful and keep focused.

Work

This card suggests that many priorities compete for our time and attention.

Three of Pentacles

The Three of Pentacles is a card that is about collaboration and teamwork. A young man stands at the entrance to a building with two other men, deep in discussion. It is clear that although he is the younger of the three, he is considered to be wiser, for he is the one that has been elevated to stand on a higher surface. Whilst he is talking, the other two are listening to him intently. What words of wisdom is he imparting to them, what information is he sharing that they will find helpful? Perhaps they have views that they want to express and which he should consider if the best course of action is going to be agreed upon.

The card speaks to us directly of prosperity through business matters. When we turn this card, we may have achieved a higher status or rank at work and, through promotion, have taken a more senior position where we are now responsible for directing and managing others. We may have developed a business idea and are now able to market it, informing people of the benefits that it will bring to them. It could be that we have found a new way of turning a creative hobby into a tangible product that we are now able to sell. Whatever it is, the card is here to tell us that now is an excellent time to share with the world the skills and knowledge that we have.

Of course, we have only just started the journey. When we are in a place to market our business idea or have just taken a more prestigious position at work, we still have much to learn and much to do. Just as now is the time to share our experience with others, we can also benefit from the advice and support of other people who can help us take a few more steps forward.

Love

An opportunity will present itself to express to a partner or friend what we want out of a relationship, but we should also listen to what they need.

The Secrets Of The Tarot

Money

We may be able to advise others in financial matters.

Work

Now is a good time to progress our business idea or career to the next level.

Four of Pentacles

A man sits on a chair, concentration etched on his face. His arms are crossed tightly across his chest as he clutches a gold coin so that nobody can take it from him. He has placed two other coins beneath his feet, each foot planted firmly above each one, and has balanced another one on his head out of reach. So constrained is he by his horde that he is quite unable to move.

There are two possible feelings that we could have when we see the Four of Pentacles in a reading, and which one we feel will depend on our situation, the question we have asked, and the other cards in the spread. On the one hand, this card suggests that we have so much money that we don't know what to do with it. We have an embarrassment of riches. We may have put it in the bank or invested it in savings of another kind and are worried that if we take it out, we may waste it on items that we do not need. On the other hand, it could signify that we have just enough for our needs. Or perhaps, to put it another way, barely sufficient for our needs and are so paranoid about losing what we have that we are holding on to it for dear life.

In some respects, it doesn't matter which of the two situations are the closest, for the message that the Four of Pentacles is giving us is the same. Whichever the scenario, the card asks us to consider the purpose of money. Is it to be held on to for the sake of having money, or is it to be spent and enjoyed? The card reminds us that if we treat money with a reverence that it frankly does not deserve, it cannot bring pleasure to our lives. If we are so fearful of losing money that we do not spend it, we cannot gain anything. We cannot open our arms and grab hold of any other opportunities that the Universe may have for us.

Love

The card is here to remind us that money cannot love us back.

Money

To plagiarise a quote from the musical Hello Dolly, "Money is like manure, it is not worth a thing unless it is spread around."

Work

We may currently be battling against change, holding on to what we know, too fearful of risking a step into the unknown.

Five of Pentacles

The cards of the tarot deck are neither positive nor negative. The guidance they give can be both or either depending on the situation we find ourselves in, the question we are asking and the other cards in the spread. However, it is difficult to feel anything but overwhelming despair when we are faced with the picture in the Five of Pentacles.

A couple trudges slowly through the snow on a winter's evening, the man on crutches barely able to walk, the woman wrapping her thin threadbare shawl around her shoulders in an attempt to keep herself warm. Dejection is written on their faces, and it is clear that they are suffering and do not know where to turn. But help may yet be at hand. If we look closely at the church they are passing, there is a light on in the window. There may be people inside who can give them comfort and warmth.

When we see the Five of Pentacles in a tarot reading, the card indicates that we may be feeling a sense of material loss at this moment in time. Maybe we do not have the finances to do all we want or the resources we need to get a project off the ground. The card reminds us that in life, if we truly want something, we must keep going however hard the journey seems. That around the corner help may be at hand. It does warn us, though, against sitting back and hoping we get the breakthrough we need. Expecting the Universe to take pity on us. If we need help or support, we may need to reach out and search for it.

Love

If times are hard, we are reminded that true love costs nothing.

Money

We should not lose faith. Help may be close at hand if we take the time to look for it.

Work

It may seem like everything is against us, but there may be team members, co-workers, colleagues or others in our network who could share some of the burden.

Six of Pentacles

The Six of Pentacles is a card about both giving and receiving. When we turn this card in a reading, it is not immediately clear which one applies to us. A wealthy man is providing money to others who are in desperate need and kneeling at his feet. Is it the rich man who represents us? Are we able to give money or gifts to others we know may be in need? Or are we represented by the beggars who are forced through circumstances beyond their control to look towards others for support and help?

The message, of course, is different depending on the situation in which we find ourselves. If we are in a position to help, if we have more money than required to service our most basic needs, then the Six of Pentacles asks us to look for opportunities to do so. This may be providing funds to someone close to us to tide them over a difficult patch, a loan to someone who wants to start in business, a gift to someone going through a bad time and may need cheering up. If we cannot spare funds, the card reminds us there are always opportunities to offer our time and skills to those in need.

If our situation is reversed, the card asks us not to be too proud to ask for help when needed. It reminds us, though, that this should only be a short-term situation. We should not come to rely on the generosity and support of others, use any loan or gift wisely and look for opportunities to become self-sufficient in the future.

Love

We should open our hearts to let love enter and leave freely and without expecting anything in return.

Money

If we can give, we should do so, and if we are in a position of need, we should not be too proud to ask for help.

The Secrets Of The Tarot

Work

Skills, knowledge and experience should be shared by the many, not kept by the few.

Andrew Laycock

Seven of Pentacles

The Seven of Pentacles tells us that we will achieve our material goals in life through slow, steady, diligent progress. Now is not the time to rush headlong towards our dreams, nor try to grab whatever life offers us. Instead, it is to work carefully, thoroughly, taking regular breaks to keep ourselves fit and healthy, for there is no point in achieving success if we are not well enough to enjoy it.

In the picture on the card, a man leans on his rake, having collected most of his gold coins into a neat pile. There is still some work to do. We can see that there is one gold coin still to be raked, but it was hard and tiring work, and he now needs to rest awhile and admire what he has done so that he is refreshed for the work that is still to do. Of course, he is tempted to continue, to get the job done quicker, but to do so would mean that his work would not be as neat, and he may tire himself out.

When we see the Seven of Pentacles, it is a warning that we should not push too hard or rush too quickly in our quest to achieve the material success that we desire. The Universe will reward us for the hard work we have done when the time is right, when we have mastered the skills that will bring us success, when we have the right attitude and temperament to treat material success with the reverence and care that it deserves. We are on the right path, but there is further work that we need to do. That work should come later, though. For now, we need to pause, recharge our batteries for the journey ahead and reflect on the journey we have travelled so far.

Love

Now is the time to focus on what we love about our partner above all else. If we are single, we should consider the qualities we want from a partner and keep those in mind.

Money

The Secrets Of The Tarot

Time is a much more precious commodity than money.

Work

The card reminds us to strive for a work-life balance. There is no point in pushing for success if we are too burned out to benefit from it.

Eight of Pentacles

The Eight of Pentacles is a card about hard work and dedication to a task. In the picture on the card, we see a young man, an apprentice, busying himself with the task of making gold coins. He has completed six of them, they are of a very high standard, and he is justifiably proud of them. They are hanging on the post now so that anyone who passes can see and admire them. He hopes if they like them enough, they will offer to buy one from him and pay him a reasonable price. So confident is he in the quality of his work that even though he has them still for sale, he is continuing to make more. He concentrates hard on his work, knowing that he does not need to look for customers. They will stop when they see what he has for sale.

The Eight of Pentacles is the natural progression of a project or job from what we saw in the previous card. In the Seven of Pentacles, we were encouraged to pause, reflect on what we have completed and identify what we need to do next. In the Eight of Pentacles, we have now decided what needs to happen and got down to business, working on the detail and the specifics of our project to achieve success.

The card is a reminder that when a job needs doing, we should do it to the best of our ability. It may be that we take on extra responsibility at work without complaint. We work hard to ensure that both our current role and the additional responsibilities are completed to a high standard so that in the fullness of time, the work is recognised and rewarded. It may be that now is a time for us to learn a new skill or gain new knowledge through study, which will enable us to achieve a better job. The Eight of Pentacles shows us that sometimes in life, we should work on something without the expectation of reward in the present because this will lead to a greater reward in the future.

Love

The card reminds us that sometimes we can find love when we least expect it.

Money

When we see this card, we are asked to remember that money doesn't grow on trees. We must work for it.

Work

If we put in the effort now, we will be rewarded in the future.

Andrew Laycock

Nine of Pentacles

Now is the time to sit back and enjoy the fruits of our labour. Or is it? A woman stands dressed in fine robes amid her vineyard, a pile of gold coins at her feet. She is looking around her, admiring the scene. In the distance, we can see her house standing in all its grandeur. There is much to love, for the vines are lush, green, and plump with fruit.

Much hard work is necessary to develop a thriving and productive vineyard. The work starts in the cold of winter when each vine must be painstakingly pared back, so only two twigs are left. The vines need to be nurtured throughout the winter and the early spring, protected from the harsh weather and the animals and insects that prey on their first buds. As we move into late spring and summer, the vines should be trimmed, thinned out, often using the moon's energy so that all the power can be focused on the growth of the fruit. And in the heat of the summer, the vineyard is at its most beautiful.

But of course, there is still hard work to be done. The grapes will not harvest themselves. When we see the Nine of Pentacles in a reading, it tells us that although through hard work we have got to where we are, we shouldn't stop for too long. If we want to continue to reap the rewards that life has given us, we need to continue working hard at it. Just as one cold spring, or wet summer, can ruin a harvest, if we take our eye off the ball, we too can suffer and lose everything we worked hard to attain.

Love

We should not take for granted what we have right now.

Money

Now is the time to enjoy what we have earned or gained, but we should put some aside for a rainy day.

The Secrets Of The Tarot

Work

When we attain what we want from our careers, we should look for further opportunities to progress.

Andrew Laycock

Ten of Pentacles

An older man sits outside an archway that leads into what appears to be a thriving and bustling town. He is surrounded by his family and looks on with obvious enjoyment as the next generation chat and plays, secure in the knowledge that he has adequately provided for them and can now rest and relax in his old age.

We are all hoping for this ideal if we have a family. As we move through the phases of our own life, and at the same time, give life to, nurture and support the generations that follow, we will know before we shuffle off into the next world that we provided our family with everything they needed. The Ten of Pentacles is a lovely card to get in a reading because it means just that. It is a card of accomplishment. We have attained everything we set out to do both for ourselves and others and can now sit back and take it easy. It highlights the importance of not focusing on material wealth to the exclusion of everything else. The older man, although undoubtedly rich, is not enjoying his wealth because of the money he has made, but because the money has enabled him to ensure his family are comfortable, secure and happy.

The key message in this card is that money does not make you happy. It is what you do with it that counts. In the short term, happiness may come from material possessions, a new car, a piece of jewellery, a designer bag, but in the long term, these count for nothing. The card asks us to continually ask ourselves why we want to achieve our material dreams. Is it for the satisfaction of being rich and having everything we want, or is it because of the difference we can make?

When we turn this card, it tells us that we will have the opportunity to achieve everything we need in life. Note the use of the word need rather than want because, as far as material possessions are concerned, the suit of pentacles reminds us to keep our feet on the ground. When we have achieved what we need, we will be faced with a choice. As the older man in the picture, we can sit back and enjoy it, or instead start again. We do not have to stop, but we may choose to. The choice is up to us.

Love

The importance of family relationships is highlighted in this card.

Money

We will attain everything we need in life, but it is worth nothing if we don't help those who mean the world to us.

Work

The card tells us that we have achieved everything we set out to do. We can now sit back and enjoy what we have attained or start again on a new project or career. The choice is ours.

Page of Pentacles

When we see the Page of Pentacles, it is a sign that we are at the start of a journey to manifest our dreams into material wealth in the real world. Interestingly, unlike many of the cards in the suit of pentacles, the primary focus of our attention when we see the Page may not be money or material possessions but in attempting to achieve something worthwhile. This may be developing a hobby we have into a creative commercial enterprise, the intention to learn a new skill to enhance our career prospects at some point in the future, or it may be developing our knowledge to be more informed about a subject that interests us. We are starting on this journey because we enjoy doing it, or we believe it will expand our minds, but just because money is not our driving force in starting the journey, it does not mean we won't have attained it by the end. Rather than an expectation, the material success we achieve will be a bonus because we do what we want to do.

When we meet the Page of Pentacles, he is standing in a lush green meadow staring wistfully at a gold coin in his hand. The dreamy look is because the attainment of money seems a long way off. He can see it and touch it, but he does not yet have it in his pocket to spend. We should pay particular attention to the placement of this young Page's feet. One is placed firmly on the ground whilst we can see that the other is barely touching it. He needs to remember, as we do, that in the attainment of our dreams, we need to keep our feet firmly on the ground and take small steps along the path, not allow them free rein to take flight. The warning in this card is that to succeed in our endeavours, we must make plans, have a clear structure and a goal and not overextend ourselves. Eventually, success and, with it, wealth will come.

Love

Although it may not seem like it, what we do now will help us find love at some point in the future.

Money

Material wealth will come through doing something that we want to do.

Work

When we see the Page of Pentacles, we are likely to start to learn a new skill or expand our knowledge in some way to enhance our career or business prospects.

Knight of Pentacles

The Knight of Pentacles sits atop his sturdy carthorse in the middle of a field surveying his land. We sense from the stillness of the picture that he does not need his armour, that he is not in any way under threat. All is calm, but he is wearing it anyway, for he knows no different. It is the way of the Knight to be always prepared, always ready for battle.

Of all the Knights in the tarot deck, the Knight of Pentacles is the one that is most true to the Knights calling, the one who is most determined to protect his lands at all cost. The card is one of protection, safety and security and when we see this card in a reading, it tells us that now is a time to conserve what funds we have, spend only what we need and save the rest. We should not try to make any dramatic changes to our financial situation now, even if we are struggling financially, because to do so may lead to us taking a risk. Now is a time to continue to do what we have always done whilst taking every opportunity to put as much money aside as possible.

On a mundane level, when we see the Knight of Pentacles, we may well be feeling as though we are stuck in a rut, working hard but seeing no real benefit from the work we are doing. The Knight empathises with our situation but asks us to persevere. We will make steady progress and receive everything we deserve through hard work.

Love

We may feel as though we are stuck in a rut but now is not the time to try and make changes.

The Secrets Of The Tarot

Money

Now is a time to save, not spend.

Work

It may feel like we are working hard but making no progress. Success will come in time.

Andrew Laycock

Queen of Pentacles

When we are introduced to the Queen of Pentacles, we see her sitting on her beautiful throne surrounded by all manner of earthly possessions. In her hand, she holds a gold coin. Her throne is decorated with carvings of angels, fruit, trees and animals. The throne is placed in a lush green meadow filled with plants and flowers, all at the peak of their natural beauty. At her feet, a rabbit leaps into view, even he does not feel threatened because he knows that there can be nothing here to harm him. She is the archetypal earth mother, queen of all the beauty on earth.

When we see the Queen of Pentacles, we are reminded that not everything of value has a price. We can be rich in life without having vast resources of money. The scent of a beautiful flower, the taste of a home-cooked meal that has been made with love, the touch of freshly washed cotton sheets on our body as we sleep, the time to sit quietly and do nothing. All these experiences can hold a value far above any material possessions we may own. The queen tells us that the pursuit of money is all very well, but we should not pursue it at the expense of other experiences in life.

On a mundane level, the Queen of Pentacles can represent a trusted advisor we may need to connect with regarding our finances. All the court cards in the tarot deck are gender-neutral, so this could be male or female. We should not believe that it is a woman just because the queen has appeared. Maybe we need to consult an accountant or financial advisor who can support us with help and advice about business or financial matters. The queen represents wisdom, so we should never shy away from asking for advice when we need it.

Love

We should aim to spend some quality time with a special someone in our life, maybe by going for a walk together or arranging a date night.

The Secrets Of The Tarot

Money

The card reminds us that not everything of value has a price.

Work

We can enjoy even the most mundane task if we undertake it with care.

King of Pentacles

In Greek mythology, everything King Midas touched turned to gold. When I see the King of Pentacles in a reading, I am always reminded of his story. If any king in the tarot deck represents the attainment of financial success and material wealth, it is the King of Pentacles.

When we meet him, he sits on his imposing throne in front of his castle. His robe is richly embroidered with a design of vines plump with fruit, and in his hands, he holds a golden sceptre representing power and a golden coin representing wealth. He has achieved much financial success in his life and is determined to keep it and use it wisely.

The King of Pentacles is a card that represents financial security through either business, investment or property. It shows us what we can achieve through careful investing and sound financial management. The King of Pentacles has not got where he is in life by taking risks, gambling or spending his money on material possessions that give him pleasure in the short term but do not add anything to his life in the long term. What he has achieved he has done by adopting a cautious but progressive financial strategy where every step of the way has been carefully thought through and analysed. Everything that has been spent has been done so for a reason. He urges us to do the same.

On a mundane level, the King of Pentacles represents a banker or tax adviser that we may need to consult or approach if we have excess money to invest. We should invest in traditional investments, not "get rich quick" money-making schemes. If we are starting in business or own a business, the card suggests that we need to ensure strong foundations are in place if future success is to be assured.

Love

Love needs to be constantly worked at if long term happiness is to be assured.

Money

The king urges us to build a strong foundation for a secure future.

Work

The actions we take now will decide our future success. We should choose what we do with this in mind.

We have now completed our journey through the prosperous pentacles. The story helps us to understand our relationship with material possessions. It provides us with an insight into how we can work with money to live a prosperous life. Let us summarise what we have learnt from each of the cards.

The Ace of Pentacles brings us a gift so that we can start our journey to a prosperous life.

The Two of Pentacles urges us to balance our money to have enough for our needs and the commitments that we have made.

The Three of Pentacles celebrates our success so far and asks us to share our success with others.

The Four of Pentacles asks us to carefully consider the purpose of money and our relationship with it.

The Five of Pentacles talks of financial loss but tells us that help may be at hand if we only dare to search for it.

The Six of Pentacles asks us to give freely if we have plenty and accept readily if we do not.

The Seven of Pentacles explains that success will come through slow, steady progress.

The Eight of Pentacles reminds us that through hard work and dedication to a task, we can achieve what we set out to do

The Nine of Pentacles reminds us that there is still work to do although we have achieved much.

The Ten of Pentacles shows us the true value of money.

The Page of Pentacles reminds us to keep our feet firmly on the ground.

The Knight of Pentacles asks us to preserve and protect what we have.

The Queen of Pentacles tells us that not everything of value has a price.

The King of Pentacles urges us to think of the future as we live through today.

The Swords That Strive

Also known as arrows, blades, feathers and scimitars, the suit of swords tells of the actions that we need to take when faced with decisions. It is not an easy suit, and when we see several swords in a reading, it suggests that we face conflict, challenges, and struggles in our lives. That there are some decisions that we need to make before we can move forward. These may be painful to us or others. We may find the decisions burdensome and difficult to make. To overcome them, we may have to place a higher value on logic over emotion, fact over feeling, analysis over intuition, which may not be natural to us. We may feel uncomfortable at times, but the swords are there to protect, guide and offer advice. They are our friends, not our foe.

The suit of swords has fourteen cards in total, an ace, or the first card, through all the numbers to ten and then four court cards, Page, Knight, Queen and King. The cards each give a different insight into the decisions we need to make to overcome challenges or conflicts in our life. As cards of the minor arcana, they highlight mundane matters instead of life-changing events, so when we see a card in the suit of swords, it is more likely to signify minor challenges rather than a major crisis. Let us now look at what guidance the Swords that Strive can give us when they appear in a reading.

Ace of Swords

Aces always signify the start of something new, and the Ace of Swords is no different. When I see the Ace of Swords in a reading, I am constantly reminded of the phrase "to the victor the spoils". A hand grips the sword tightly, the sword itself is held upright, representing firmness and clarity. We see a gold crown draped in a laurel wreath at the tip. We have emerged victorious from whatever battle we have faced.

But hold on a minute, I hear you say. We haven't fought any battles yet, for we are only at the start of our journey through the suit of swords. This is very true, but the victory of which we talk is a battle that has been raging in our minds or our hearts for a while. Suddenly when we see the Ace of Swords, like a master strategist who, when planning a war campaign, sees with clarity how the battle can be won, we too have realised what we need to do to overcome a challenge. The Ace of Swords signifies a breakthrough in our thought process over a decision or a problem troubling us. Like a lightbulb being switched on above our head, we know the decision we need to make, or the action we need to take, to solve whatever it is that has been causing us such consternation. It could be a way to restructure our finances to save more money for the future. We could have thought of a way to encourage a child to revise for an exam that they were not interested in, a conversation we need to have with our other half over an equal and fair distribution of household chores. Whatever it is, we now know exactly what we need to do.

When the Ace of Swords appears in a reading, it means that decisive action now needs to be taken. Any words that are spoken need to be precise. The card warns against ambiguity or pussyfooting around. We need to meet whatever situation we are faced with head-on, state our expectations, undertake our actions confidently and assuredly. If we do, we will emerge victorious.

Love

We have realised a decision that we need to take regarding a relationship, or if we are single and want a relationship, we have decided what we are now going to do to get one.

Money

We know what we need to do to put our finances on a firmer footing.

Work

The solution to a problem that has been troubling us suddenly becomes clear.

Two of Swords

A woman sits still as the night that surrounds her on the shores of the lake. Her arms are crossed, and in each of her hands, she holds two swords pointing in opposite directions. The weight of the metal in her hands is as reassuring as it is burdensome, for she knows that if she needs them, they will offer her protection. She hopes that won't be necessary, for she has come here to be alone, and she does not want to be disturbed by either friend or foe.

When we see the Two of Swords in a reading, it means that we are at this moment in time avoiding a decision that we know we have to take. This could be because the decision is not an easy one to make. There are too many variables, too many unknowns, and we need time to think. Equally, it could be because although we know what the decision needs to be, we are avoiding it. After all, it will impact different people in different ways, and we cannot balance everyone's needs. We may be hiding from the decision, frightened of making it and taking solace in our current situation, for if we stay here, it is safe. Nothing changes, nobody gets hurt. The problem, of course, is that we cannot stay here indefinitely. The longer we wait, the heavier the burden of the swords will become. Our limbs will get stiff and inflexible, we will find it even more challenging to move. The longer we wait, the more complex the decision will become.

The card asks us to remove the blindfold from our eyes, which prevents us from facing the decision, uncross our arms, put down our swords which weigh heavy in our hands and make the decision that is such a burden to us at this present time. In doing so, we should try and be fair to ourselves and those around us, although we should accept that sometimes this is not possible. If it isn't, as long as we have tried we will not have failed. The only failure is not making the decision, because ignoring it does not make it go away. If anything, the situation may worsen.

Love

The card tells us that we may need to make a decision that we do not want to make. In doing so, we should consider both parties feelings and needs.

Money

We may be struggling to balance our income and expenditure. We know how to change the situation, but we do not want to, because to do so may mean we have to take action that we do not want to take.

Work

We are trying to balance too many commitments at work. We need to prioritise, but in doing so may have to give up on activities that we enjoy.

Three of Swords

Whenever the Three of Swords turns up in a reading, it is accompanied by a sharp intake of breath from whoever is next to me at the table, and sometimes even an exclamation of horror or an expletive or two. The poor Three of Swords is an oft-misunderstood card and, for this reason, has got an awful image that is entirely undeserved. Very few people want to see it, mainly because they don't fully understand what it signifies.

The Three of Swords is one of the simplest illustrated cards in the tarot deck. A large red heart is suspended in a cloudy, rainy sky, pierced through the middle by three sharp swords. Whenever people see it, they automatically assume it means the end of a relationship, the death of a loved one, a divorce, a betrayal. Still, as we know, the suit of swords does not explicitly represent love, so why should this card signify the end of love? Swords represent decisions or the solution to a problem primarily. Rather than assuming the card means we have a broken heart in the context of a love situation, we have to look deeper into the symbolism to find the true meaning of this card.

Now don't get me wrong, even though the card does not signify a broken relationship, it is not a fantastic card to get in a reading because it does suggest heartache of some kind. Truthfully, tarot cards are neither positive nor negative. They offer guidance, advice, and learning, but when we see the Three of Swords, it suggests that we are going to have to make a decision that is not going to be pleasant. One which will cause us a certain amount of emotional angst. The card signifies that an emotional attachment to a situation is clouding our judgement, that we feel we cannot win because whatever we do will cause us a certain amount of hurt or pain. It may be, for example, that we have a great working relationship with two colleagues at work who we manage, and a job opportunity has arisen, which means that one of them can be promoted. They are both excellent at their job, and both want the promotion, and although both deserve it, we know that we will have to choose one over the other. It could be a more painful decision closer to home, such as a much-loved pet that is ill. The vets have told us that there is nothing further that they can do, and we know the kindest thing would be to let them move on to the next life, but we don't want to. Maybe our children have left home, and we know the sensible thing now is to downsize our house, but we are too emotionally attached to it and the memories that it holds to decide to put it on the market. We know we have to make the decision, but we avoid it because we know the outcome will be painful.

When we see this card, it is worth remembering that if there is no loss, then there can be no rebirth. If there is no hardship, we can't learn. If we have not suffered, then we do not understand great joy. Heartache is only temporary, and although it certainly cannot be enjoyed, it is sometimes necessary to move on.

Love

A decision needs to be made that may temporarily break our hearts.

Money

We may need to cut back on expenditure that we feel is necessary, but what we think is essential may be a luxury.

Work

We may have to give up on something special to us, such as a development opportunity or a career move that we accept we do not have the skills for at this time.

Andrew Laycock

Four of Swords

On first looking at this card, the obvious interpretation that we come to is that a Knight has died, but this is not necessarily so. The stone outline of a Knight lies on a tomb in church, a sword horizontal below and three swords hanging suspended in the air pointing downwards at the head. The tomb may be empty. Preparations may have been made for the time when after a long and prosperous life in which many battles have been fought, the Knight will be able to rest before he starts his journey into the next life.

Swords, of course, as we already know, represent decisions, so the battle the Knight has fought are decisions he has had to make, or problems that have had to be solved. When we see this card, it tells us that we have recently made a decision, solved a problem, overcome a difficulty, and now can rest after the challenge. This is important; we cannot go through life finding solutions to one problem after another without causing ourselves stress or paying the price on our health or emotional state. A Knight does not move from one battle to another without taking the time to rest, and nor should we. There will be many problems to face in life and numerous decisions but now is not the time. Now is the time to hand the burden to someone else and enjoy a break from decision making.

Of course, we may ask how it is possible to rest when decisions are to be made, and this is where the warning in the card lies. So often in life, we feel that we are the ones who have to make the decision. That the responsibility is ours and ours alone. This card reminds us that we do not walk this journey alone, just as the Knight has others he can turn to for support, so there are others in our life who also need to take some of the responsibility. And we need to turn to them occasionally to ensure we do not pay the ultimate price for taking too much of the burden on ourselves.

Love

Now is the time to go with the flow.

The Secrets Of The Tarot

Money

We should enjoy what we have, regardless of whether we have a lot or a little. If a decision needs to be made, let others make it for us.

Work

The card tells us to make no decisions at this time regarding work or business-related matters.

Andrew Laycock

Five of Swords

The Five of Swords is a card about winning and losing, although arguably, we could equally say it is about losing and losing. The victor stands in the foreground as his enemies walk away in defeat, but if we look closely at the victor's face, we can see that he takes no pleasure in the win. Perhaps he has realised that the effort of the battle was not worth it for what he has gained, or maybe he feels that he has lost more than he has won.

When we turn this card in a reading, we have come to a decision and found a solution to a problem troubling us, but we can take no pleasure in the decision we have made. This may be because in finding a solution, we have had to give up on something important to us, or we know the decision will impact others negatively. Perhaps it is a choice we have been forced to make where neither solution was advantageous or favourable.

So often in life, we have to make decisions that have no positive outcome. It could be that our son has asked, yet again, for a loan of money, and we do not want to give it to him because it is clear that he is not managing his finances properly. To loan him the money will not help him in the long term because it is not teaching him a lesson, but if we decide to say no, we know he will not be able to pay his bills, and we do not want to see him struggle. Maybe we have been negotiating a pay increase and have managed to get a slight increase, but now our company feels differently about us because it is not something they wanted to pay. Perhaps we have been in conflict with our neighbour over a minor parking dispute and have proved that right is on our side, but if we are now not speaking, if a good relationship has now soured, we may be asking ourselves if it was worth it.

When we see the Five of Swords, it is an indication that we have overcome a problem and finally found a solution, but if the cost is too high, then truly it could be said we may have won the battle but could well have lost the war.

Love

In a relationship, one person's needs override the others, causing conflict and frustration.

Money

Financial issues lead to decisions that prioritise some commitments over others.

Work

We may feel that we are being taken advantage of.

Six of Swords

Despite the sense of sadness depicted on this card, the Six of Swords is quite an uplifting card filled with faith and hope. We see a young man struggling to row a woman and child single-handedly across the sea. The woman's head is covered as she does not want to see where she is going, but if she only took the shawl away from her face, she would see that the waters they are rowing in are much calmer than those they have left behind.

What can we learn from the Six of Swords? The key message is one of hope. We have made a decision, and because of this decision, we will find life much easier in the future. We are now in a state of transition, leaving behind the troubles that have defined our most recent weeks and months and sailing into much calmer waters where we should begin to feel much more positive. Note the use of the word should, for the card does provide us with a warning. It reminds us that life will not be easier or more fulfilling if we continue to carry the baggage of our most recent experiences with us. To gain the maximum benefit of the next few weeks, we must rid ourselves of the negative thoughts weighing us down.

We may have had financial troubles and decided to downsize our home to release the equity, but we feel aggrieved that we now need to live in a smaller house. In doing so, we completely forget the enjoyment we can squeeze out of life without the burden of a large mortgage. We may have changed jobs, given up our high-powered job in the city for a similar role in a local firm and are annoyed at our loss of status and salary, whilst forgetting how much more time we have to enjoy with our family. The Six of Swords urges us to look at the benefits, not the downsides, and embrace the positive aspects of change.

Love

We may feel battered by our recent experiences, but life will get easier if we can only rid ourselves of the baggage we are carrying from the battles that we have fought.

Money

Easier times are coming. We should enjoy them and not be fearful that we may make the same mistakes again.

Work

If we keep working as we have, we will get the break we deserve.

Andrew Laycock

Seven of Swords

Each of the tarot cards holds many secrets. It is impossible in a book such as this to cover every possible meaning of each card, as each meaning will reveal itself dependent on the question we have asked, the situation we have found ourselves in, or how it relates to the order of the cards in the spread.

As with all cards, the Seven of Swords has multiple meanings. I will cover a couple of the most obvious ones here, as these are the ones that provide us with guidance and advice in the majority of cases.

First, let us remind ourselves what the picture on the card shows us. A man sneaks away from a military camp, having stolen five swords. He has left two swords behind, either because he could not carry them, or because he was in such a rush to get away without being caught that he forgot them. As we already know, the primary focus of the suit of swords is one of the decisions, so the most straightforward interpretation when we see this card is that we have taken a decision that was not ours to make and, in doing so, have not been able to consider all of the facts. This could be because we didn't have them, or because we did not take the time to find them out, or we felt we instinctively knew the answer without looking into the problem too deeply. Regardless of why this is, the card holds a warning that, like the thief who soldiers have seen in the background, we could well be caught out because, ultimately, the decision was not ours to make.

Of course, this assumes that we are the thief in the picture. What if we are not the thief but one of the soldiers in the background? When we draw this card, it could be that we have allowed someone to decide for us, leaving us with a solution that we do not want. Perhaps we had bought a new car with the understanding that we had a choice of colours but didn't read the small print in sufficient detail and on paying the deposit, we found that the price we have paid only covers three options. We have found that we still have a decision to make, but we don't have

The Secrets Of The Tarot

the decision to make that we thought we had.

Whether we are the thief in the picture who has taken a decision that was not ours to make, or have had a part of the decision taken from us, the card urges us not to let this happen in the future. It encourages us to take our responsibilities seriously and treat decisions with the reverence they deserve.

Love

We may be tempted to jump to conclusions and make a decision when we do not have all of the facts.

Money

The card warns of making decisions around money without considering the implications.

Work

If we are not alert to what is happening around us, someone else may get work, business or the credit that by rights should be ours.

Eight of Swords

A woman is held prisoner, trapped in the centre of a cage of swords. Her arms are tied behind her back and her eyes blindfolded so she cannot see where she is or how she can get out. When we see this card, it signifies that we are trapped by indecision. We have decisions to make, but we literally cannot make them, either through not seeing the decision we have to make or because we are in denial about the problem or a situation we are in and cannot see a way out.

Usually, when we are unable or unprepared to make a decision, it is a problem, but when we see the Eight of Swords in a reading, our indecision is a blessing. How can this be, we may wonder, because surely if we have a decision to make the common-sense approach, would be to make it. This is very true in most cases, but this card is the Universe's way of telling us that our decision-making process is flawed at present. That we are too blinkered or too wrapped up in a situation to make the right decision objectively and fairly to move forward. I liken this state of mind to being unable to provide advice to a child about their relationship that seems to be in difficulty, because the love we feel for them prevents us from being objective. Or on a more mundane level, spending hours and hours trying to decide where to go on holiday when the reality is we shouldn't go anywhere because we have no spare money.

When we see this card, it is a reminder from the Universe that we should open our minds to all possibilities, and only when we can do so will we be able to see the way forward. We may not want to. After all, like a career criminal who is unable to survive in the real world for long, we may find our self-imposed cage the safest place to be. But we cannot stay here long. If we do, we may lose the ability to decide in the future, and we cannot pass control over to others completely without losing our sense of purpose or happiness.

The Secrets Of The Tarot

Love

Our feelings blind us to make an objective decision.

Money

Trapped by circumstances beyond our control, we may feel forced to make a decision that is ultimately not in our best interest. The Universe is telling us now is not the time to try and solve this particular problem.

Work

Too many responsibilities are leaving us unable to see clearly. Pause for a while. The decisions can wait.

Nine of Swords

This is the card of sleepless nights. A woman sits up in bed in the dead of night, holding her head in her hands. Behind her, nine swords are displayed, signifying the magnitude and complexity of the decision that has disturbed her sleep and woken her up.

For some reason, our troubles always seem magnified in the middle of the night when everyone else is asleep, and the weight of our problems are preventing us from going back to sleep. We cannot see clearly. We turn minor issues into a major crisis' or believe there can be no solution however hard we think.

If we have woken up in the night and spent a sleepless night worrying, we will also know that the likelihood is that we eventually doze off sometime before dawn. We wake up after a couple of hours of sleep, wondering why we had built the decision into such a major crisis, or with the answer staring us in the face. And this is the key message held within the Nine of Swords. It shows us that when we are faced with a decision, we should not spend too much time worrying about the problem or the many and varied impacts, for we have no control over these. Instead, we should spend our time productively, analysing the facts and the options available to us to find a solution for the actions we do have control over. The card asks us to focus on the solution, not the problem, what we can do, not what may happen. In doing so, we can have a good night's sleep and be prepared for the rigours of the day ahead.

Love

Rather than worrying about the problem, we should look for the solution.

Money

The thinking time is over. Now is the time to get our finances on track.

The Secrets Of The Tarot

Work

The card suggests that we are spending too much time worrying about work. It is easy to say, but we should try to remember that we work to live, not live to work

Andrew Laycock

Ten of Swords

The poor Ten of Swords is often referred to as the worst card in the tarot deck, and when we look at the card, we can see why many people feel this way. A man lies face down on the ground, half-covered by a cloak. Ten long sharp swords are embedded in his back, and he is obviously dead, for no one could have withstood the sort of assault he has endured and lived to tell the tale. The card signifies loss, endings and, of course, betrayal because he has quite literally been stabbed in the back.

Before we get too carried away with this card›s tragedy and melodrama, let us remind ourselves what swords mean. The suit of swords refers to decisions and solutions. When we are talking about loss, endings and betrayal, we refer to the loss of a decision, the end of a problem and the betrayal of someone in the context of the situation.

There are, of course, no good or bad cards, no best or worst in the tarot. The cards are here only to provide us with advice and guidance. The betrayal of which this card speaks is merely that a decision we have to make has been taken out of our hands. We have lost control of it, either because the Universe has decided to take matters into its own hands or someone else has made the decision for us.

Now, this could be a good or a bad state of affairs depending on the decision we have to make, the circumstances we have found ourselves in, and the decision›s complexity. Let us say that we were struggling to decide what to cook for dinner that evening, and suddenly, our partner arrives home with a takeaway. Before we scoff at this example, let us remind ourselves that the minor arcana deals with mundane matters and not every reading refers to a life-changing event. We may feel relieved, elated even, that we don›t have to make a decision. On the other hand, if we had defrosted some fish and had a fridge full of vegetables and the decision was what to make with the ingredients, we could well feel aggrieved that our partner had not thought to tell us what they were planning. Alternatively, we may have had an evening out planned for weeks and are trying to decide what to wear, when our partner phones to tell us they are working late and so we have to stay in and look after the children for it is now too late to arrange a babysitter. We no longer need to decide what to wear, the decision has gone, and we feel betrayed by our partner that they did not fight harder to leave work earlier, knowing as they did our plans.

When we see this card, we have lost control of a decision. We may be angry, bitter, and in some cases relieved, but we have nothing to fear, for there will be other decisions to make in the future.

Love

A decision about our relationship has been taken out of our hands.

Money

External forces likely impact our financial situation. This could be a financial institution that tells us they want a new repayment plan for a debt we have, a supplier who has put their costs up or a partner who has bought a new car with some of our joint savings.

Work

A decision has been made that impacts our work about which we were not consulted.

Page of Swords

In the story of the three little pigs, the wolf huffed, and he puffed as he threatened to blow the poor pigs houses down. The pigs can see and hear who the enemy is and take steps, some more successfully than others, it has to be said, to thwart him. When we meet the Page of Swords, he, like the pigs, is ready to battle against an enemy, but unfortunately, he cannot see who the enemy is. If indeed there is an enemy at all.

The Page of Swords stands on high ground where he knows he can defend himself from any enemy who may try and get close. The wind is blowing strongly, ruffling his hair and pulling at his clothes, and he has got hold of his sword, ready to strike at anyone blown in on the wind. There is no one there, though. He is expending energy that he doesn't need to, that he could conserve for another time.

When the Page of Swords appears in a reading, he shows the risks and dangers of making a decision too quickly. We find out a piece of information, hear part of a story, see a situation begin to occur. Before waiting to find out how it will develop or taking any time to analyse the information we have heard, we jump in and make a spur of the moment decision.

Of course, when we do this, we may strike lucky. Our aim may be true, the decision is correct, but we can also quickly get it wrong, strike at thin air, and miss the mark. The Page highlights our impetuous side and asks us above all else to think carefully before we rush to make a decision. After all, one may not be needed, or it may not be ours to make.

Love

We are seeing problems where there may be none. We need to be cautious, for if we look too hard, we may cause the problem ourselves.

Money

Try not to rush to find a solution to a financial situation, for a solution may well present itself in due course.

Work

Decisions made without a careful analysis of the facts can testify to our skill and knowledge. Or be a lucky guess.

Knight of Swords

The Knight of Swords rushes into battle eagerly. He holds his sword aloft, ready to strike down anyone who fights against him. Between his legs, his trusted steed carries him forward. He will not let him down even if he does not entirely agree with the course his young charge is taking.

The Knight of Swords represents either a person we know who has strong values and ideals, or qualities that we possess ourselves. If it is the latter, values are everything to us, and we will promote them and defend them at all costs, even if the consequences of our actions cause hurt or difficulties to those we encounter. When the Knight appears in a reading, he suggests that we may have rushed into a course of action because we instinctively believe it is correct, without thinking through the possible outcomes that may result from the action we have taken. Let us say that one of our values is timekeeping. We hate being late. We think tardiness is unacceptable and cannot be excused or explained away. We get caught in traffic on our way to see a friend we have arranged to meet for lunch. Rather than call our friend to explain the situation, after all, we cannot do anything about an unexpected traffic jam, we spin the wheel, drive out of the queue and down a road close by, hoping that it will take us in the right direction. If we believe that birthdays should be celebrated, we may arrange a surprise party for our daughter's birthday even though we know she hates parties and have no idea whether she has plans. It is all very well to have strong values and beliefs, but the Knight of Swords urges us to consider other people's needs as well as our own, to think objectively about a situation rather than pursue a path that seems right but may not be logical.

Love

If we are in a relationship, we should consider the other person's needs as well as our own. If we are single, we should be realistic. The perfect man or woman does not exist.

Money

The card suggests that we are not being realistic about a financial goal, that to continue on the path we are on could be reckless.

Work

In a work-based situation, it is better to learn to walk before attempting to run.

Queen of Swords

Firm but fair is always the expression that comes to mind when I see the Queen of Swords. She sits on her throne, imparting justice, making decisions, sharing her wisdom and advice with anyone who needs it. Many may consult her for they know her judgements will be sound and based on a solid analysis of the facts, but few may enjoy the experience. She does not suffer fools gladly, and her decisions may not give you what you want, although they will undoubtedly help you find what you need.

The Queen of Swords, like all the court cards, may represent someone with who we come in contact, or highlight characteristics that we have. On a mundane level, she may suggest that we need to consult someone in the legal profession, or who works for a government body for a judgement, to make a ruling or a decision on a matter that we cannot resolve. We may not necessarily like the answer we receive, but we can be confident that whatever they decide will be fair.

If the card highlights characteristics that we have, it suggests that we may be called upon to make a decision, and in doing so, we will need to consider all the facts and speak to everyone who may be involved before we do. It may take us a while to make a decision, there is no way of rushing the Queen of Swords, but once we have made a decision, we stick to it, even if others may want us to reconsider. We can be sure there is no flip-flopping around or ambiguity when this card appears.

Although the Queen of Swords considers all the facts and will only make the decision after careful analysis, she will not explain the rationale behind her decision. Unlike the other queens in the tarot deck, the Queen of Swords is shown in profile. There is always a side of her that she keeps hidden from all but those who she most closely trusts.

Love

The Queen of Swords suggests that we may need to take advice from

The Secrets Of The Tarot

someone else who is not as close to the situation as we are.

Money

We may need to sit down and carefully and objectively analyse our financial position to move forward. Decisions may need to be made that are not pleasant.

Work

The card suggests that our work will be appraised and that how we have performed will determine our future.

Andrew Laycock

King of Swords

Sometimes in life, when a decision has to be made, we are caught slap bang in the middle of it. At other times we are on the outside looking in.

When we see the King of Swords in a reading, it is a sign that we need to detach ourselves from the situation or circumstances that we find ourselves in to make a logical, rational decision where emotions have been taken out. It may be that we are in the middle of a family dispute where our partner and child are at loggerheads with each other and are expecting us to be the referee, each of them putting their side of the story to us so that we can make a judgement in their favour. Perhaps we have a choice to make at work. We have been working on two projects that have advanced to such a stage that our boss wants us to devote all our time to one of them. Both interest us, we have invested a lot of time and energy in them, and it is difficult for us to choose one over the other. It could be that we are unhappy in our relationship and need to broach the subject with our partner, who we think is equally sad, but we are scared to, for we think things may be said in the heat of the moment on both sides that will cause pain. When this card appears, it is a sign that we need to step away, take some time out, look at the decision from outside, for it is difficult to see clearly what we need to do when we are trapped in the centre of the problem or situation.

If we are asked to judge a family argument, we should hear both sides and then leave for a few hours, go shopping, take ourselves for a coffee, go to the gym. There we can think about the situation uninterrupted before returning with our decision. If we are asked to decide which project we want to continue developing at work, we should take the weekend to think about it, maybe go for a walk or a run so that our minds aren›t cluttered with work-related matters. If we are in the centre of an unhappy family relationship, then now is the time to take a break, treat ourselves to a spa weekend or if this is too expensive, ask to stay with a friend for a few days. Away from the stress and the arguments and the bitterness, we can contemplate our future and, in the short term, decide what we want to say.

On a mundane level, in the same way that the Queen of Swords suggests that we may need outside help, when the King of Swords appears, he also may suggest we need to get professional advice. The difference between the King and the Queen, though, is that we are asking for a judgment with the Queen. We are asking for advice to make the ruling ourselves with the King.

Love

We need to be careful not to say things in the heat of the moment that we will regret. We should take ourselves away from the situation for a day or two to think carefully about what we want to say.

Money

It is difficult to decide when we are at the centre of the problem. However hard it may feel, we should try and detach ourselves from the challenges we face to make a decision. If this is impossible, we should get outside advice.

Work

We should not make hasty decisions that could affect our long-term future. It is always reasonable to ask for some time to think.

We have now completed our journey through the Swords that Strive. The story helps us understand the battles that we have to fight to make the decisions to overcome the problems in our lives. The suit of swords is not an easy suit. When they appear, they often warn of conflict, challenges and struggles, but they give us the guidance we need to help us overcome life's challenges. Let us remind ourselves what they tell us:

The Ace of Swords brings us the answer we have been searching for to a problem or challenge.

The Two of Swords urges us to make the decision that we are avoiding, for it will ease the burden that we are carrying.

The Three of Swords warns of heartache to come but reminds us that sometimes these decisions must be made in life.

The Four of Swords asks us to rest to replenish our energy, we have overcome one challenge, but there are battles still to come.

The Five of Swords tells us that sometimes we are forced to make a decision which will mean there are winners and losers, and sometimes only losers.

The Six of Swords talks of happier times ahead if we can only lose the baggage we have carried so far.

The Seven of Swords explains the consequences of making a decision, not ours to take.

The Eight of Swords warns us that our decision-making process is flawed at this moment. We should make no decisions until we can see the way ahead clearly.

The Nine of Swords tells us that there is little point in worrying about what may happen when we can use the time more productively.

The Ten of Swords reminds us that though we may have lost control of this decision, there will be other decisions in the future that we will be able to make.

The Page of Swords warns us of the risks of making a decision too quickly.

The Knight of Swords warns us of the consequences of basing decisions solely on our ideals and values, but has little expectation that we will heed the warning.

The Queen of Swords tells us that a fair judgement is made after carefully analysing all the facts.

The King of Swords urges us to take ourselves away from a situation or a problem so that we can make a clear decision.

The Working Wands

Depending on the deck we are using, wands can also be called batons, bows, rods, staffs, or staves. They are an action suit representing fluidity and motion. They focus on the activities and tasks that we complete on a day-to-day basis. They relate to work and business but not the traditional sense of going out to work. It can be any work we do, from small tasks at home like preparing dinner or cleaning out the cupboards to the significant roles we take in life such as mother, friend, co-worker, boss. When we see wands in a reading, especially if we see several wands, they suggest that we are currently involved in an activity of some sort or another.

The suit of wands has fourteen cards in total, an ace, or the first card, through all the numbers to ten and then four court cards, Page, Knight, Queen and King. The numbered cards each give us a different perspective on any activity or task we are undertaking, and the court cards suggest how we may be feeling as we do the work. Let us now look at what guidance the Working Wands can give us when they appear in a reading.

Andrew Laycock

Ace of Wands

I always think of this card as the relay card. If you follow sports as I do, and in particular athletics, you will be familiar with the relay race where a team of runners take it in turns to run around a track holding a baton before handing it over so that the next person can take their turn. They are working in competition with other teams, and the team that gets all of their runners around the track first without dropping the baton wins. In many respects, this symbolises the Ace of Wands' meaning. The universe is handing us a task and telling us it is now our turn to take it forward and make it our own.

Of course, this means when we see the Ace of Wands in a reading that we have a job or a task to do whether we like it or not. We may not have wanted this job or expected to get it. We may not think that it is our responsibility to do it, but we have been handed it to complete and complete it we must. Whether we want to do it or not is not essential. It is irrelevant. We have to do it, take ownership and see it through either to the end or to a point where we can hand it over to someone else. There is no shirking away from it. The job is ours now.

Because it is ours, though, we do have a choice. The task may have been started, there may be a plan that we are expected to follow, but we are now the one in control, and we can shape it, mould the task or activity to meet our ideas. If the job has been started, we can choose whether to build on what has been created, amend what has been done or discard it and start again. We can decide to do what is expected of us or grow it into something much bigger. We can stretch ourselves or do only what is necessary to meet the primary objective. We can decide whatever we want, but we cannot ignore it, for others depend on us now.

Love

We may find we have to work at our relationship, or work hard to find one if we are single.

Money

The Ace of Wands has a double edge to it. It can signify a new source of income, or equally, depending on the other cards around it, a further expense.

Work

We have been given a new job to do.

Andrew Laycock

Two of Wands

"He's got the whole world in his hand, he's got the whole wide world in his hand, he's got the whole world in his hand, the whole world in his hand".

When we see the Two of Wands, we cannot help but think of this well-known hymn, sung in the version I remember by a choir of over a hundred members in perfect harmony. When we see the card, we can see that a man stands on the shores of a large lake, looking ahead of him to a distant horizon. There are mountains in the background, and he is standing between two wands, positioned solidly in the ground. He holds a globe of the world in his right hand, symbolising the external forces at work in his mind. He is not thinking internally, but externally, not thinking small but big. In the world at large, we may be small and insignificant, but my goodness, we are a giant in our minds.

The Two of Wands is a card of discovery. We have much to discover about ourselves, and the world has much to learn about us. When we receive this card in a reading, it suggests that we are about to make a job or a task much more significant than it was initially planned. What was relatively straightforward will grow much more extensive. With this will come the opportunity to stretch and challenge ourselves, and we are certainly ready for the journey in front of us.

On a mundane level, the Two of Wands suggests we may travel overseas for work or come in contact with people from other countries in the nature of our work.

Love

A long-distance romance is indicated, or we may meet someone from overseas.

Money

We may need to balance our finances and be cautious about taking on too much.

Work

We may need to travel for work, or our work may involve people from other countries.

Three of Wands

At first glance, the Three of Wands is a very similar card to the Two of Wands, and to be honest, the meanings themselves are also very similar. We need to remember, though, that the tarot tells a story, and so each card can flow naturally from one to another, each sharing a different aspect of the same tale.

Like the Two of Wands, a man stares out towards a distant horizon in the Three of Wands. He cannot see what is out there, but he can certainly imagine it in his mind. When we see the Three of Wands in a tarot reading, it urges us to think big. It differs from the Two of Wands because this particular card focuses not on what we are doing now but on what we want to achieve.

The Three of Wands is a card about vision. We are looking at the big picture, the why we are doing what we are doing. We can see in our mind the end game, the completion of the task at some distant point and all the work that we are going to do to reach that goal. We have a long way to go, now we are only at the start, but we know what the end of our journey will look like. It is like building a house and knowing what it will feel like sitting in our kitchen even though we have only laid the first stone.

The Three of Wands is a very positive card as it is filled with hope, optimism and dreams of the future, but in common with all cards, it holds a warning. The man in the picture is holding on to one of the wands for support, and the tarot suggests we may also be fearful of letting go. Whilst we are only dreaming of what the distant horizon looks like now, we are safe. As soon as we let go, strike out for the distant shore, we are putting ourselves at risk of failure.
We may ask ourselves if we are ready for the challenge. The tarot says we are.

Love

A long-term relationship is on the cards, or if we are in a relationship

The Secrets Of The Tarot

already, we are making long term plans.

Money

The reward we receive for our endeavours could well be significant.

Work

We are focusing on the long-term outcome of the activity instead of the short-term steps we
are taking.

Four of Wands

The Four of Wands, above all else, is a card of celebration. When we draw this card in a tarot reading, it signifies that we should go out and celebrate life. We have much to be thankful for. If we have completed a task, we should pat ourselves on the back. If we are in the middle of an activity, we should take some time to review what we have done and note our achievements. If we are at the beginning? We have translated our thoughts and ideas into something tangible, and if that isn't cause for celebration, I don't know what is.

Fours in the tarot traditionally focus on structure and order, and so when the Four of Wands appears, it is also a sign that success will come through a structured and orderly approach. It asks us to ensure that we have clear plans to complete what we are going to do and that we regularly review these plans. Even if planning is not our strong point, we can write a list, mark off each item as we complete it, and give ourselves a reward when we pass key milestones.

On a mundane level, the Four of Wands suggests that success will come through careers in the building or property sectors, be that investment or construction. It can also mean partnerships and cooperatives; success will come through working with others.

Love

This is the commitment card and can signify marriage or the celebration of a long-term relationship.

Money

Our finances are strong, and we may consider investing in property or real estate.

Work

Things are going well for us at work, and we are likely to have a reason to celebrate. Either a promotion, increased reward or the successful completion of a task.

Andrew Laycock

Five of Wands

Five men are busy trying to complete a task. Each one waves their wand in the air as they try to work out the best way to place their wand exactly where they want it to be. The anger and frustration they feel is written all over their faces as they are constantly coming up against their opponents who want to place their own wands in the ground.

It would be funny if it wasn't so tragic, because these men are not opponents and enemies but teammates. They are trying to complete not five individual tasks but one, although anyone watching them would never believe that. If only they each stopped trying to place their wand in the ground, sat on the grass and talked to each other, they could work out what each of them needed to do. The task would be much easier. They would finish it much quicker. Will they think of doing that, or is their dogged determination to do it their way going to prevent common sense from happening?

When we draw the Five of Wands in a reading, it suggests that we are being thwarted in our task by either external influences or our own thoughts and feelings. This may be because others around us each have a different objective to achieve, and in them attempting to achieve what they want, it is preventing us from meeting our own goal. Equally, it could well be a situation or a set of circumstances that surrounds us and prevents us from achieving what we want. Our need to care for a parent or child may, for example, be taking our focus away from what we want to accomplish in a work-related matter. We may be struggling to match the two together, but rather than spend time thinking of an alternative plan, it could be that we are trying to achieve both in tandem with disastrous results.

The Five of Wands is a card of frustration, conflict, and competition and can typically be seen negatively. Tarot cards, though, are neither positive nor negative. They merely try to guide us to what we need to do. When we draw the Five of Wands, it is a sign that now is not a time for action but discussion, that to continue on our current path will result in chaos, whereas if we stop and assess where we are, we may find a way that leads to order. The choice, as always, though, is down to us.

Love

There may be competition over a love interest.

Money

There are many competing demands for our finances.

Work

We are facing competition. Other people have their own motives. We need to tread carefully but stay true to our values.

Six of Wands

Following on from the chaos and confusion of the Five of Wands, the Six of Wands is a card that shows us what can be achieved if we take a different path. Rather than going it alone, the Six of Wands tells us that through working together as a team, victory, success and recognition for a job well done can all be ours. It is a card of strength, success and achievement. We have achieved what we set out to do, and not only are we pleased with the result, but those who we asked to help us on the way want to celebrate with us.

This can be seen almost as the exact opposite of the Five of Wands. Whereas in the previous card, chaos reigned as we worked alone, in the Six of Wands, order and success is achieved through working with others. It is too simplistic to imagine that this is a card where the key message is one of teamwork. When we draw the card, it asks us to consider who can help us and what we need to do to ensure that others can help us on the way. For success to be achieved, we must know where we are going, and if others are to help us, they must know this too. Communication, planning and a focus on results are all messages that we need to take from the Six of Wands if successful completion of a task is to be assured.

The Six of Wands can be seen very positively, but it does hold a warning that if we have achieved through the help of others, we should recognise and reward those who have helped us. If we don't, then they may not be as prepared to help us if we need them in the future.

On a mundane level, the Six of Wands may suggest that we are being rewarded and recognised for work we have done.

Love

Our partner wants the same things as us. If we are unattached, we may meet someone who has the same outlook on life as we do.

Money

We should expect an increase in fortunes, either through promotion or someone who wants to invest in us.

Work

Our efforts will be rewarded. We will be recognised for what we do.

Andrew Laycock

Seven of Wands

In the picture on the Seven of Wands, we see a man standing at the top of a hill, fiercely defending his position against an unseen enemy. Anger is written on his face as he furiously stabs his wands into the ground behind him to stake his claim over the land he believes is rightfully his. So busy is he in his task that he has not noticed his foolishness in wearing odd shoes. He was in such a rush to climb the hill before anyone else that he did not have time to check that he was dressed correctly.

The Seven of Wands demonstrates our weaknesses and fears when we are completing a task. We are precious about what has been done and how it has been done. We do not want anyone to challenge us or suggest that we could have done it differently. So quick are we to maintain the status quo that we have been careless and neglected our other duties. Rather than look around us to find out what else needs to be done, what assistance we can offer others, we are only bothered about our task and maintaining what has been completed.

When we draw the Seven of Wands in a tarot reading, it can suggest that we are completing a task how we have always done it without trying to identify whether or not there is a better way. We are focusing on what we know, taking safety in what we have always done, refusing to allow anyone else to suggest a different way of doing something. It is often seen as a blockage card as we are closing our minds to other opportunities or ideas, and because of this, we could open ourselves to failure or ridicule.

There is, of course, a positive aspect to this card, and that is when we draw it, depending on the situation we find ourselves in, it could indicate that we are prepared to stand up for what we believe in with courage and conviction. We are ready to put our necks on the line and defend what we believe is right even in the face of adversity. Whether positive or negative, the Seven of Wands shows us that we are passionate about what we are doing, and what we can achieve, even if others are not prepared to support us.

Love

We may not be prepared to compromise in a relationship, or if we are looking for love, we may be too focused on the past to find new love.

Money

We are unwilling to change our approach to money and may have unrealistic expectations.

Work

We are digging our heels in and are not prepared to change, even though it may be in our best interest to do so.

Andrew Laycock

Eight of Wands

The Eight of Wands is one of the simplest illustrated cards in the tarot deck. The picture shows eight wands flying through the air, in parallel, towards the ground. The angle of the wands as they hurtle through the air suggests speed and strength; it is clear that they have been thrown with some force.

When we see the Eight of Wands in a reading, it indicates that what has been started cannot be stopped. The wheels have been set in motion. The decision has been taken, so we must now see what we have initiated through to completion, regardless of whether we want to or not. The universe has decreed that is the way it will be.

Fortunately, the Eight of Wands is generally seen as a positive card. The wands are perfectly in line with each other, suggesting that all the different threads that have led to the activity or task being undertaken complement each other and work well together. There is a structure to our job that is helping the goal to be achieved, and we are confident that when completed, we will be happy with the result. The Eight of Wands tends to appear when the hard work has been done; the wands are angled downwards, meaning we are over the worst are now moving towards the result.

In common with all tarot cards, even though it can be seen positively, the Eight of Wands can hold a warning, and that is that we may have lost control of the task. If we throw something into the air, we lose control of where it will land. It is the same with the activity we are working on. It has taken a life of its own. Even if we wanted to stop, if, for instance, we decided that the result was not going to be worth the effort, or our circumstances had changed, there is an inevitability to this card that means whether we want it or not, we will get what we wished for.

On a mundane level, the Eight of Wands can suggest that we may need to travel for business by air, and that the trip will be successful.

Love

We may be tempted to push too hard for commitment or for our partner to change.

Money

We could have been spending a lot recently, or are about to spend a lot. Our spending could get out of control.

Work

We may have been busy at work, but we are past the worst. This card can also signify travelling for business.

Nine of Wands

The Nine of Wands is a card that focuses on our fears and insecurities. A man has placed his wands in the ground behind him to make a fence. There is one last wand to place before he completes his task, but he is clinging to this final wand because he is scared of taking the final step. He dare not finish the job as he is worried that the result will not live up to his initial expectations.

When we draw the Nine of Wands in a reading, we need to ask ourselves what we are afraid of. Is it that we believe that when we take the final step to complete the task, we will have nothing left to do, that once our work is done, we will no longer be needed? Are we scared that once we place the final element in its rightful position, what we have achieved will not be what we expected or hoped for? After all, sometimes we may feel that it is better not to have achieved than to have completed our task and think that we have failed and not fulfilled our early promise.

If we receive this tarot card, it is a sign that we are being urged to complete what we have started. Whatever the outcome, whether it is what we expected or not, we need to draw a line under it. We cannot move forward if we do not finish the activity. It will constantly be on our minds, gnawing at us. It will be the niggling doubt asking us at various low points in our life, what if? So what if what we have completed is not what we wanted or hoped for? We can always start again, make changes, adapt for next time. There is no point in us doing all the hard work to let ourselves down at the last moment. We should be brave and take that final step; we never know we may end up being pleased with the result after all.

Love

Something is lacking in our relationship, and we need to identify what. If we look for love, the card suggests we are afraid to take the final step.

The Secrets Of The Tarot

Money

We need to look at ways to improve our financial situation. There is no point in pretending what is happening isn't happening.

Work

Work may seem challenging, but we have to finish the task at hand even if we believe it will not deliver what it needs to or expect.

Ten of Wands

When we draw the Ten of Wands in a spread, the Universe is giving us a sign that our responsibilities burden us. A man carries in his arms ten wands, they are cumbersome and awkward to move, and he is stooped low with their weight in his arms. If we look closely, though, we can see that he has chosen to pick the wands up and carry them in that way, nobody has forced him to do it, and there could well have been an easier and more manageable approach that he could have taken.

When we see this card in a reading, we need to ask ourselves why we have taken on so much. Is it because we like to feel the burden of responsibility deep down, or do we not believe anyone else can do the task as well as us? The tarot is giving us the message that although we may have a lot to do, we have chosen to do it. We have taken on the task ourselves.
Of course, this suggests that the Ten of Wands has a negative connotation, but in truth, as we already know, no card in the tarot deck is purely negative or positive. We can look at the card positively as it shows us that although we are hard at work, the task has almost been completed. In the same way, as a farmer will gather up his harvest and take it to market to sell, so we have gathered up the wands that we have created and put them to good use in the way they were intended.

The Ten of Wands has a lesson for us in common with all tarot cards. The tarot wants us to ask ourselves if we have to shoulder the whole burden of responsibility for completing the task or look around us to see if others can help or have resources that we can use. Of course, it could be that we like to be under pressure, but even though we want to be busy, our body does occasionally need a rest.

Love

We may be going through a tough time emotionally at the moment.

The Secrets Of The Tarot

Money

We feel overburdened and stressed about money, and that it is all down to us.

Work

We have taken on too much, but is this because we had to, or felt we had to?

Andrew Laycock

The Page of Wands

The Page of Wands represents the start of a new project or activity. He is a free spirit, creative and untamed, and when we meet him, we see him standing in the middle of the desert, a wand covered in new buds in his hand. The wand represents the seed of an idea that he is determined to take forward. He has recognised the opportunity it contains and is eager to get on and make something of it. He is passionate, committed. There is a fire in his soul.

There is a restlessness about the Page of Wands, and when we draw this card in a reading, it tells us we are eager to get started and make quick progress. We are going to throw ourselves into the task or activity with enthusiasm. Nothing is going to stop us. If we are working alone, it suggests that we are about to enter a period of frenetic activity where we make things happen with boundless energy. If we are working with others, it indicates that we will sell them our idea and persuade them to follow us.

The Page of Wands is a get-up-and-go sort of card and is typically seen in a very positive light, but it holds a warning in common with all tarot cards. It asks us to be careful not to commit all our resources to the task at hand too quickly. We may be enthusiastic, but our idea is still fresh and not fully developed. If we go too fast, we may make mistakes and cause problems. The tarot does not want to temper our enthusiasm. It just wants us to be mindful that sometimes there needs to be less haste and more speed in any activity.

On a mundane level, the Page of Wands may suggest that we are about to start a new job or start a new course of study and learning. We may feel the need to prove ourselves to others, but the tarot urges us to remember that we are beginning a journey and still have much to learn.

Love

It is time to take a chance on love, or if we are in a committed relationship, time to add something different.

Money

Opportunities are in abundance when we receive this card. If we are only brave enough to take them. We should not, though, expect immediate returns.

Work

An incredible work opportunity is on its way to us, which could well be better than we hoped.

Andrew Laycock

Knight of Wands

The Knight of Wands charges into view, his wand held aloft, his horse rearing up under the power and the speed with which the Knight moves forward. The Knight has little consideration for how his horse feels. He is focused on where he is going and getting there as quickly as possible. How he gets there is not something he will consider.

The Knight of Wands is the natural successor to the Page. When we see the Page of Wands in a reading, this suggests we are about to start our journey to turn our idea into action. When we see the Knight, it usually means that we are in full throttle. Nothing can stop us now.

The problem, of course, with the Knight of Wands' approach, is that the speed with which we are moving forward means that we are not fully in control of what we are doing. If activity and action always translates into success, then we would be sure to succeed, but unfortunately, this is not always the case in life. We are not rewarded for effort but results. The story of the Hare and the Tortoise comes to mind. It is not the quickest, nor the one who expends the most energy that succeeds but the one who can stay the distance. We would do well to remember this lesson when the Knight of Wands is drawn.

Love

Do not rush to judgement, or if we are looking for love, we should not pounce on the first eligible person we see.

Money

Our finances are strong at the moment, but we should still resist impulse buys that we may not need

The Secrets Of The Tarot

Work

We are determined to succeed, but at what cost?

Andrew Laycock

Queen of Wands

When I see the Queen of Wands in a reading, I always think of Queen Elizabeth II of Great Britain. The Queen of Wands is the most hard-working of all the Queens in the tarot deck, and she takes her duty and responsibilities very seriously. She does not let anything get in the way of what she feels she needs to do. She may not feel particularly well, and she may have things going on in her life which makes it difficult for her to fulfil the task she has been given, but she does not let that stop her. Just as Queen Elizabeth II has devoted her life to serving the people of the United Kingdom and the Commonwealth, the Queen of Wands has dedicated her time to the task or activity she has been asked to do.

When we see the Queen of Wands in a tarot spread, she is there to remind us that we must give our all to the task at hand. Others may depend on us, and we should not let them down. If we have something to do, it is essential that we dedicate ourselves to it, that we do it to the best of our ability and skill. It suggests a period of hard work is about to start, but if we apply ourselves to the task, we will be happy with the outcome because we will achieve what we have set out to achieve. Nothing worth having is attained quickly, but the tarot tells us that we have nothing to fear, our efforts will not be in vain, our hard work will be rewarded.

On a mundane level, the Queen of Wands suggests that we will be given increased responsibilities either at work or at home. It may signal that we are about to get a promotion at work, or it could suggest that we have additional responsibilities at home.

If there is a warning with the Queen of Wands, it is that we need to be careful not to take on too much. In thinking we must help others, we may over commit ourselves and try to do more than we can manage. As we never want to let anyone down, this can lead to us feeling anxious, stressed and put upon.

Love

We feel comfortable with our situation. No changes are necessary.

Money

We may feel that we must help someone out, but we should not be tempted to give more than we can afford.

Work

On a professional basis, work is going well, we are highly thought of, but this could lead to others having unreasonable expectations on what we can do. We need to be careful not to take on too much.

Andrew Laycock

King of Wands

The King of Wands sits on his throne, holding a wand firmly in his hand. He is clothed in a cloak decorated with the lion and the salamander, symbolising strength and fire. He is the epitome of fiery energy representing the blazing sun from where the earth takes its power. His is a very positive card to get in a reading because it tells us that we are sure to succeed through dedication to the task at hand.

The King of Wands represents great strength and leadership. When we see the King of Wands in a reading, he suggests that we are going to take an idea and make it our own. We will turn the concept into reality, but we will do it in our own way. We are going to find our own unique path. He is very creative and very good at what he does, and when he appears, especially when he appears as an outcome card, he suggests that we are going to fulfil our full potential.

The King of Wands appearance is a sign from the universe that now is the time to be brave and go for what we want. The King tells us that we have every right to believe in ourselves. We just need the confidence and the chance to show the world what we can do. Success is assured when we see the King of Wands, although, as with the Queen of Wands, success will not be achieved by sitting back and doing nothing, but by hard work and dedication to the task at hand. If we apply ourselves, we will be rewarded. If we don't, we could have missed out on a great opportunity.

On a mundane level, the King of Wands suggests that we will be recognised for the work that we have done. We may well be rewarded at work by a bonus or by promotion, or if it is a task that we have done either at home or in the local community, we will get recognition for what we have achieved. The King is also often the sign of celebrity. Whilst it may not signal our name in lights, it could be that our name appears in a newspaper or a trade publication or our local library where we are recognised for what we have done.

Love

This card suggests great passion and excitement in matters of the heart.

Money

This card signifies great wealth will come through hard work.

Work

We are highly thought of and likely exert a considerable amount of influence.

We have now completed our journey through the Working Wands The story is one of action and adventure, it can signal hard work and difficulties but ultimately ends in achievement and recognition.
The Ace of Wands tells us it is our time to take action now.

The Two of Wands reminds us there is a world to discover.

The Three of Wands urges us to think big.

The Four of Wands says we have much to celebrate.

The Five of Wands asks us to work together for the common good.

The Six of Wands shows us that much can be achieved when we do.

The Seven of Wands warns us not to get too fixed with one way of working.

The Eight of Wands tells us that what has been started must be completed.

The Nine of Wands asks us not to be too fearful of finishing a task.

The Ten of Wands reminds us that the responsibility does not always lie with us.

The Page of Wands says we are eager to get started on a new activity.

The Knight of Wands suggests nothing can stop us now.

The Queen of Wands tells us that it is our duty and responsibility to dedicate ourselves to the task.

The King of Wands urges us to use our power and influence wisely.

We have now finished our journey through the tarot. The secrets have been unlocked and I hope that you have enjoyed this book. Remember that the tarot cards provide a guide to help you live your life, and they can be consulted whenever you have a question and want to open your mind to possible solutions. Unless they are in the hands of a psychic with a sixth sense, who will use the cards to help them gain clarity on your situation, they do not predict the future. In your hands they inform and guide but never tell.

Andrew Laycock is a writer and trainer. With a deep knowledge of both the Tarot and Feng Shui he utilises his knowledge to help others gain an insight into their lives.

© Andrew Laycock 2019. All rights reserved.

Any redistribution or reproduction of part or all of the contents in any form is prohibited without the express written permission of the copyright owner. You may not, except with the express written permission of the copyright owner, distribute or commercially exploit the content. Nor may you transmit it or store it on any other website or other forms of electronic retrieval system.

Published by Firehorse Ltd

Andrew Laycock

www.ingramcontent.com/pod-product-compliance
Lightning Source LLC
Chambersburg PA
CBHW060154050426
42446CB00013B/2827